Hamlyn all-colour paperbacks

John F. Milsom

Armoured Fighting Vehicles

illustrated by John Batchelor

Hamlyn · London
Sun Books · Melbourne

FOREWORD

In recent years a large number of books have been published on the subject of armoured fighting vehicles, which reflects an ever growing interest. This interest may take one of several forms – such as military history, automotive technology, modelling or merely a desire to study the development of fighting vehicles in general. For this reason a wide range of books have become available, ranging from tactical studies, regimental histories, highly technical papers, or merely volumes listing and illustrating various types of machines.

The object of this book is not to cover comprehensively the vast subject of armoured fighting vehicles. This could never be adequately achieved in one volume. It is intended mainly as an introduction to the subject, being an attempt to acquaint the novice with all the intricate factors which have contributed to the development of fighting vehicles and armoured warfare.

J.F.M.

Published by the Hamlyn Publishing Group Limited
London · New York · Sydney · Toronto
Hamlyn House, Feltham, Middlesex, England
In association with Sun Books Pty Ltd., Melbourne

ISBN 0 600 30104 4

Phototypeset by Filmtype Services Limited, Scarborough
Colour separations by Schwitter Limited, Zurich
Printed in Holland by Smeets, Weert

CONTENTS

HOW AND WHY THE TANK EVOLVED

The concept of the tank is by no means recent, and no individual man, or even nation, is justified in taking credit for its fruition.

Before attempting the difficult task of defining the tank and the whole spectrum of other armoured fighting vehicles which have come into being, it would be of value to consider the basic requirements of any self-contained fighting unit.

The oldest and most elementary fighting unit is, of course, the unarmed man. Let us take a look at the boxer, for example, and describe the qualities which enable him to defeat his opponent. After consideration one comes to the conclusion that he must possess three basic attributes: a) the ability to punch hard and knock out his opponent, b) the stamina to stand up to punishment and last out the fight, and c) the agility to fence with his opponent.

It may be argued that a

Armoured vehicle concepts of the Middle Ages. The centre vehicle (*above left*) by August Rommeli (1588) was an amphibious concept.

boxer with a powerful punch and great agility might, under certain circumstances, be adequately suited to achieving his aim in that he can avoid being hit altogether. When this is so, he needs only the stamina to last out the fight and not necessarily that to stand up to punishment. Such a situation represents only a more complex combination of these three factors, as will be seen later. In military terminology, these three characteristics receive new names:

a) Firepower;
b) Protection;
c) Mobility.

Although these are the prime (or explicit) requirements in warfare, there are a number of related (or implicit) requirements also. Such implicit requirements are that the boxer should receive adequate training and experience to fight in the most efficient manner. When one considers groups of such fighters engaged in some form of combat, the problem becomes even more complex. There are three basic types of situation: a) when both opponents are static, b) when both opponents are moving, and c) when one opponent is mobile and the other static. The outcome may depend upon quick communication between each member on a particular side or his knowledge of the size, strength and deployment (activity) of the opponent. Another important factor is the manner in which each commander groups his forces and whether he is defending or attacking.

The walking fortress, a German concept by Holschuer for an artillery-armed mobile military city (1588).

When selecting our men for a force, however, we are mainly concerned as to the extent of their firepower, protection and mobility. We would like to possess a number of men who have all three characteristics to a high degree. Ideally, one might say therefore, that the most efficient fighting unit is that which has the *greatest* firepower, protection and mobility. Since, as far as known science allows, firepower and protection are represented by devices possessing weight, we find the greater the firepower or the greater the protection, the greater the weight. It is therefore obvious that mobility will suffer.

Let us return to our boxer. In the case of a heavily-built boxer we can see, therefore, that although he might possess the stamina to survive punches and the strength to floor his opponent, he is not sufficiently agile to manoeuvre around the ring and reach him. He also quickly tires and is therefore not able to operate for sustained periods of time. If we represent the three basic factors by the sides of a triangle, we have in this case the situation of figure 1. Here, one can see that the increase in firepower (punch) and immunity (stamina) have resulted in decreased mobility (agility). As a result:

$$\text{MOBILITY} : \frac{1}{\text{FIREPOWER}} : \frac{1}{\text{PROTECTION}}$$

Fig. 1

Fig. 2

Fig. 3

Fig. 4

In the same way it may be argued that a boxer with great stamina and agility but poor punch (fig. 2), or great punch and agility but poor stamina (fig. 3), is likewise at a disadvantage. The ideal arrangement then is where the triangle is equilateral, i.e. all three factors are equally represented (fig. 4). Generally mobility is expressed as the ratio:

$$\frac{\text{POWER}}{\text{WEIGHT}}$$

or, the power-to-weight ratio. The higher the power-to-weight ratio the faster the system will move and the more capable it will be of ascending slopes. Without a certain minimum power-to-weight ratio (in the absence of some cumbersome, impractical gearing system), a system will not move at all.

Throughout the history of military science there has been a continual effort to achieve a balance between the three factors, although, at times, the circumstances may make an unbalanced system necessary. We have seen

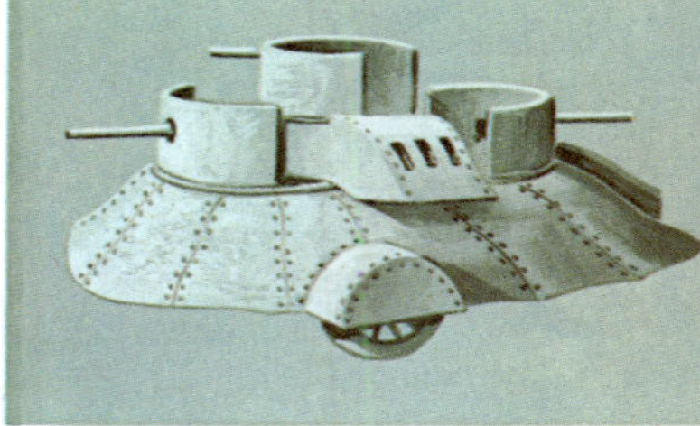

Some other early concepts for armoured vehicles. The second from the bottom, by Simms, was actually built.

The drawing above shows the universal railroad by George Kale (1825), the earliest track concept recorded.

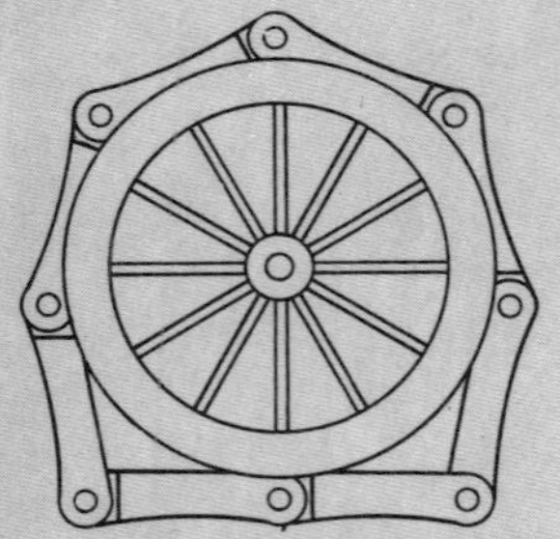

(*Above*) Gomper's tracked wheel (1831); (*below*) Clark's animated wheel (1891).

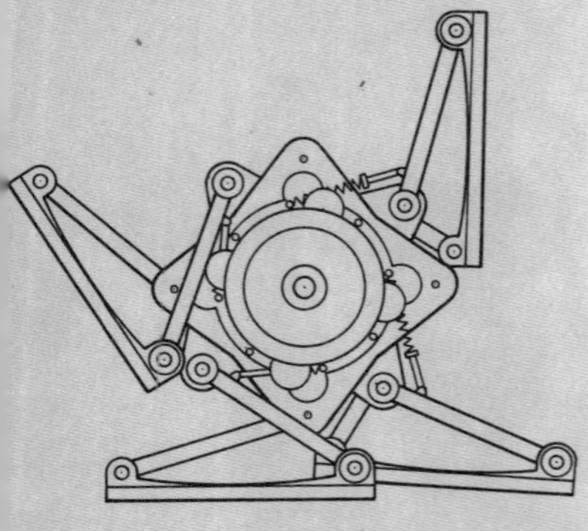

earlier that one can achieve protection by virtue of agility – the idea being to avoid being hit. The earliest battles therefore involved two basic types of fighting unit: the infantryman and the cavalryman. The ancient Persians were the first to exploit armed cavalrymen. The role of the cavalryman was to use his mobility and speed to close with the enemy quickly and penetrate his position without being hit himself: his mobility being provided by the horse. Once he had disrupted the enemy, however, it was the role of the infantry to occupy ground, engage in hand-to-hand combat with individual defenders, storm obstacles, etc. This could not be adequately fulfilled by a man on a horse.

Since there was no available means of providing sufficient power-to-weight ratios, the early infantry possessed virtually immobile devices in order to provide the firepower/immunity aspect as a supplement to the cavalry's mobility. Such devices were termed 'siege engines', and were not necessarily weapons but often protective platforms from which other types of weapons could be used.

From experiences of

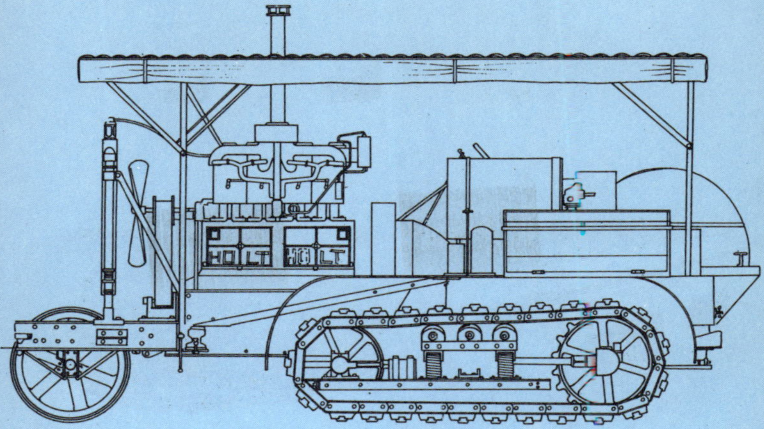

These two pages show early proposals for traction across country. (*Above*) an early Holt tractor; (*below*) Dunlop's walking wheel (1861).

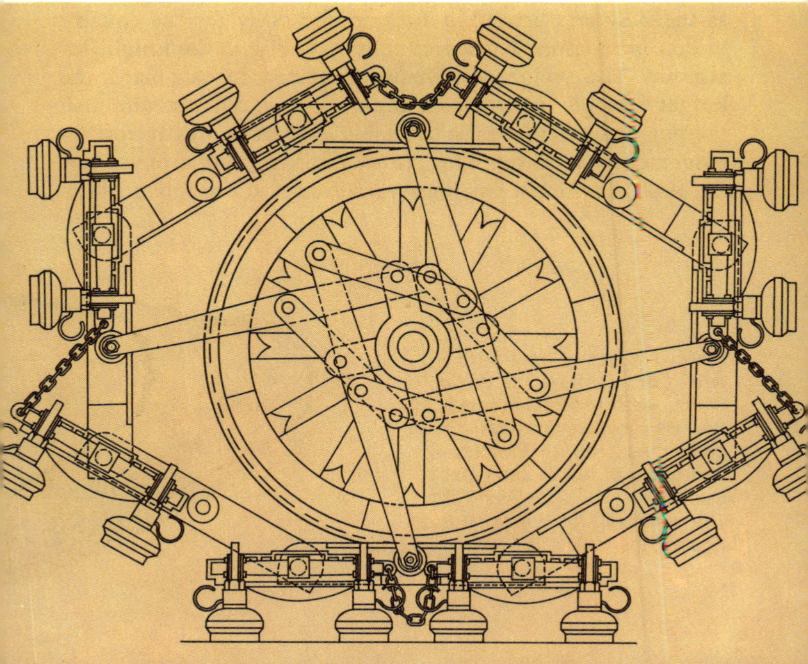

weapons that could hit cavalrymen at fairly long range (such as the bow and arrow), it became necessary for the cavalry to don protection. This eventually gave rise to the knight-in-armour. The weight of armour required to safeguard the knight and his mount from these missiles did not diminish the power-to-weight ratio to such a level as to greatly restrict movement (mobility). The era of the knight-in-armour was the first in which a weapons-versus-armour race took place.

Embryo stages of the British tank: (*above*) the 'Little Willie', which was the first armoured tracked vehicle ever to be completed. (*Right*) 'Mother' – forerunner of the British tanks used during the First World War. The wheels at the rear were used to steer the tank.

The archers made stronger bows (longbows) with greater accuracy, penetration and range, which perforated the light armour of the cavalryman. The infantry, in general, were deployed behind barricades of spears embedded in the ground with their tips facing the enemy. In consequence, the cavalry donned heavier armour and adopted modified tactics, and so the cycle continued. Eventually armies possessed so-called 'heavy cavalry' in which the knight was so overladen with armour (and also, of course, his mount) that he had to be saddled with the aid of a jib. If unhorsed by a pikeman, or by any other means, he lay helpless on the ground at the mercy of the enemy infantry.

Many standard works attribute the decline of the knight-in-armour to the introduction of firearms; this, however, is not strictly true. If we compare the performance of the gun and the longbow at that time we come to some surprising conclusions:

THE GUN	THE LONGBOW
heavy;	light;
slow rate of fire;	high rate of fire;
dependent on availability of munitions;	virtually independent of munitions supply;
short range;	long range;
low accuracy and penetration except at very close range.	accurate at greater ranges, penetration about the same.

What, then, was the reason for the adoption of the firearm?

The standard British and German tank models of the First World War: (*above*) the British Mark IV tank; (*below*) the German A7V. At this time the German name for tank was *Schützengrabenvernichtungpanzerkraftwagen*, which meant, literally, 'protected trench annihilation armoured vehicle'. The British Mark IV was the most numerous Allied tank, but only a handful of the German model were produced. An improved model of the A7V later appeared, called the A7V-U.

There were probably two reasons: firstly, it was a ready-loaded weapon, which gave the advantage at short ranges, and secondly, its less bulky form allowed it to be used at close quarters. In all events, there was certainly no apparent improvement on the ability to down a knight-in-armour. Indeed, it is interesting that prior to the introduction of the repeating rifle (e.g. the Winchester type) of the late nineteenth century, there was every reason for continuing the use of the bow and arrow as a back-up weapon. One can postulate on the effect that the archers of Agincourt might have had on Napoleon's troops at Waterloo, for example.

The first recorded case whereby the value of armour was questioned was in the fourth century AD. The Gothic horsemen who invaded the Roman Empire compelled the Roman infantry to become more mobile. The infantry could only achieve this by discarding their armour. (The most fundamental changes in cavalry tactics may be attributed to Genghis Khan.)

In Europe body armour (chain mail and scale armour) was adopted. By the Middle Ages armour was so taken for granted that entire armoured armies were formed, a classic example being that of Charlemagne during his invasion of Italy. The importance of armour at this time can be seen clearly in two respects: firstly, during his reign, Charlemagne prohibited the export of armour from his realm, and secondly one of the prime goals of the Viking raids during the ninth century was the capture of armour. Armour became much improved, but only at the middle of the thirteenth century did plate armour begin to appear. The sophistication of armour became the trend in the fourteenth century, but thereafter the value of armour began to decline. The reason for this may be indirectly attributed to the introduction of gunpowder on the one hand, but also to tactical and strategical development on the other. The introduction of the cannon put an end to isolated sovereignties, since it enabled the destruction of fortified castles without great expenditure in equipment and personnel. As a result, kingdoms increased in size and, therefore, so did armies. Consequently, armies could not afford the luxury of armoured knights and the latter, in their original proportions, would have made little contribution to the out-

The most striking American tank developments of the First World War: (*above*) the Ford 3-ton tank. This vehicle was produced during 1918 and the intention was to swamp the front with thousands of such vehicles. With the cessation of hostilities, however, all production was halted, at which time only 15 had been completed. (*Below*) the 'Liberty' Mark VIII tank. This was an American vehicle developed from British designs, which utilized British-made armour plate and various accessories. Begun during 1918, production of this vehicle was also arrested at the end of the war and only 100 were completed. The latter vehicle proved to be unreliable mechanically.

come of a battle. On the other hand, it was the introduction by Gustavus Adolphus of a strategy requiring mobility and dispersion as the prime factors in war, which finally made the knight redundant.

As is so often the case, any new theory of war which produces unexpected results soon catches on. All future armies reduced armour to a minimum (e.g. Cromwell's semi-armoured soldiers), until finally, by the early eighteenth century, armour became practically non-existent. Now the cavalryman, stripped of armour and all dead weight, could move as fast as possible. Due to the slow rate of fire of firearms and his high speed, the cavalryman was very difficult to hit and once more dominated the battlefield.

In the meantime, the idea of providing some form of vehicle which could carry soldiers into battle with protection against both firearms and other projectiles was still pursued by a few advanced-thinking individuals who had to await the invention of some form of motive power other than the horse before their ideas could become reality. All efforts were, therefore, fruitless. The only available means of propulsion were the horse and windpower. The horse, like its master, was vulnerable to all types of weapons. Even when it was placed within the confines of armour, it lacked the power necessary to move such dead weight, and at the same time was not easily commanded in battle.

Any further attempt then to re-introduce the third dimen-

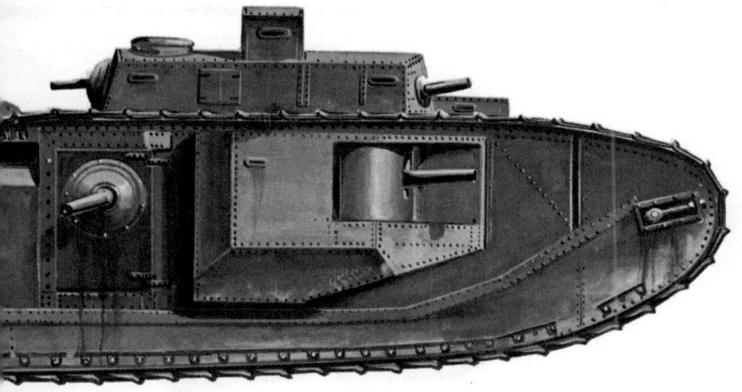

sion, armour protection, into warfare had to await the introduction of some form of engine. Apart from all this, the requirement for such a vehicle tactically was disputable; the cavalry still roamed the battlefield with little opposition, and the performance of the horse across country still takes a lot of beating even to-day! Why build such a vehicle then? Well might one ask . . . Then there was the invention of the machine-gun.

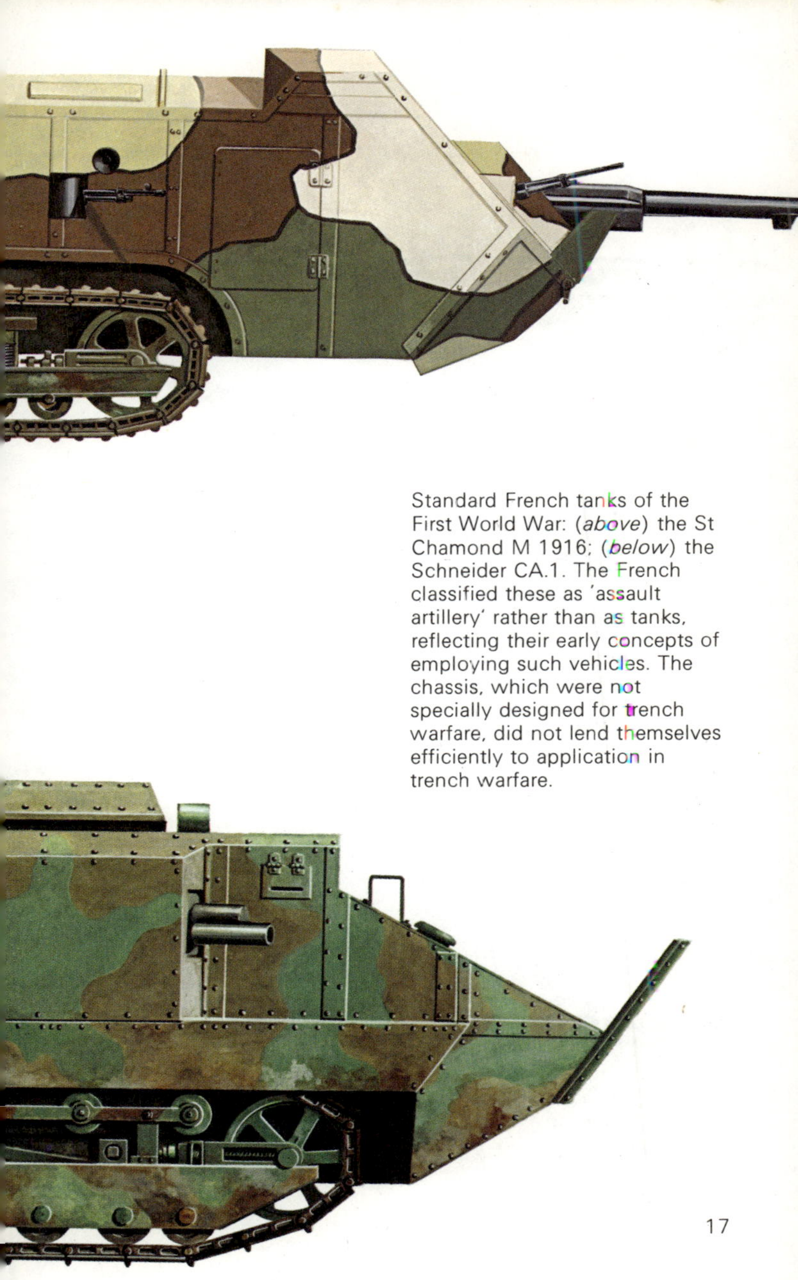

Standard French tanks of the First World War: (*above*) the St Chamond M 1916; (*below*) the Schneider CA.1. The French classified these as 'assault artillery' rather than as tanks, reflecting their early concepts of employing such vehicles. The chassis, which were not specially designed for trench warfare, did not lend themselves efficiently to application in trench warfare.

British tanks of the 'thirties: (*above*) the A-6 'sixteen tonner'; (*below*) the A-1 'Independent'; (*right*) the Vickers 'medium'. The A-6 and the A-1 were revolutionary designs which were eventually copied abroad. Both were multi-turreted and possessed a number of technical innovations. The former was a medium model for use by the cavalry whilst the latter was intended to be a mobile fortress for independent operation. The Vickers 'medium', also known as the A-2, was manufactured in quantity for the British Army from 1926 onwards. It remained the standard medium tank right up until 1938. All three vehicles took part in the experimental manoeuvres on Salisbury Plain.

The machine-gun opened up an entirely new phase in warfare. It now became possible for a relatively small number of such weapons, under concealment, to dominate the battlefield. Their high rate of fire, long range and great penetration made it virtually impossible for any form of animal – man or beast – to survive on the battlefield. That old requirement, armour protection – long ago discarded as futile and cumbersome – now became a fundamental requirement in warfare. Experiences in small localized wars at the turn of the century made this clear to many open-minded men, but the military general staff, steeped in tradition and virtually lacking any form of technical education, considered that the old means of warfare – infantry and cavalry – would still take precedence.

The inevitable result of this philosophy was the early phases of the First World War, when opposing armies, ensconced behind row upon row of obstacles and barbed-wire, faced each other across vast shell-ridden areas of terrain, the dominance of the machine-gun over which reduced the mobility factor of warfare to zero.

The idea of an armoured, high mobility vehicle provided with guns – so often proposed during preceding years – now

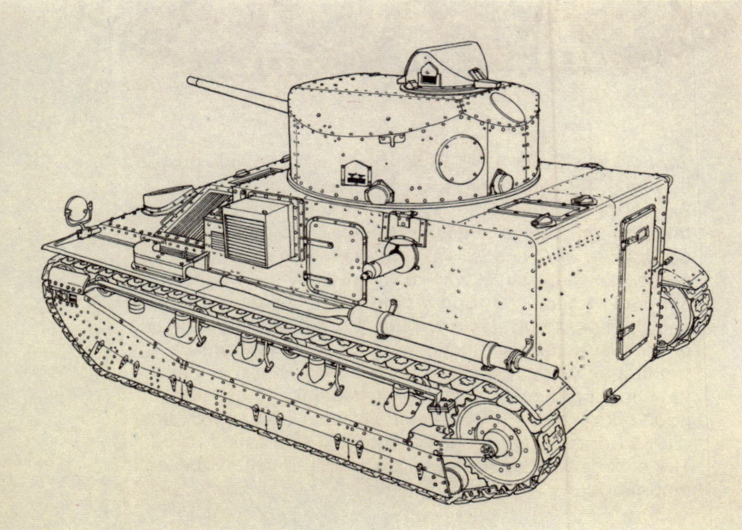

became a basic necessity. At the same time, the invention of the internal combustion engine and the development of the continuous track facilitated the effective realization of this concept. Since the appearance of such a vehicle, generally referred to as the tank, warfare has returned to its old form of combining firepower, mobility and armour protection. What the tank accomplished can be summarized as follows:

a) it increased mobility by replacing muscular power with mechanical power (i.e. facilitated relatively high power-to-weight ratios);
b) it increased protection by neutralizing the small-arms bullet with armour plate;

(*Above*) the Czech LTH.38 light tank. This vehicle proved to be one of the most significant tank developments ever. Before the Second World War, many were exported all over the world and some remain in service even today. With the occupation of Czechoslovakia by the Germans a large number of these tanks were taken over by the German armoured troops and used during the occupation of France and the Low Countries and, later, Russia. Towards the end of the war all future German light and medium tank production was to be based on the chassis of this tank, due to its low production cost, high reliability and generally good performance. The German versions (two types, either with a front- or rear-mounted engine) were called Pz.38 (d). The chassis was also used for a number of self-propelled gun mountings.

The AMR 35 (*below*) represents a typical example of a French tracked armoured car of the 'thirties. The abbreviation AMR stood for *Auto Mitrailleuse de Reconnaissance* (self-propelled machine gun for reconnaissance). All French reconnaissance vehicles were very fast, whereas the normal fighting tanks were slow vehicles intended for infantry accompaniment. Such vehicles were employed by French cavalry units. The particular vehicle depicted here was a French derivative of the famous British Carden-Loyd machine-gun carrier, but here furnished with a fully-rotating turret mounting a machine-gun, and the robust scissors-type suspension so typical of French armoured vehicles of this period.

c) it increased offensive power by facilitating the crossing of open terrain, and the carrying of effective weapons into defended enemy positions.

Actual claims to the invention of the tank have been made by, or on behalf of, many individuals over the years, and it is virtually impossible to donate the honour to any particular person, or indeed nation. These claims emerged shortly after the Armistice in 1918 when an investigation was held to award sums of money to inventors of war-winning innovations. When it came to the tank, however, there were so many claimants, all with reasonably good cases, that the decision was left in abeyance and has remained so ever since. The problem lies in the definition of the word 'invention'. Can one class drawings, ideas, models, etc., as inventions, or must

Two of the most interesting French tanks of the interwar period: (*above*) the Char D1 ('Char' is the standard French term applied to tanks), and (*below*) the enormous Char 2C. The Char D was intended as a 'fast' infantry tank and, although mechanically advanced, suffered from misconceptions about the function of tanks on the part of the French High Command. The turret carried only one man, who was required to fire, load and aim the gun, manipulate the radio set, and command the tank. The Char 2C is, perhaps, dimensionally the largest armoured vehicle ever produced. It was the ultimate extension of World War I tank philosophy. Apart from the unusual arrangement of the armament, the method of track drive and steering (through the use of electric motors) was also quite novel for that time.

there be an actual working example? Even if one stipulates the necessity of a working prototype, there are still several engineers who have equal claim. It seems to me that the most important factor has been overlooked; the production of the odd experimental model had virtually no effect upon the outcome of the First World War – or indeed any other conflict of arms. It was the realization by the British and the French of the need and value of such a vehicle, the design and production of working prototypes, and the eventual application in numbers to a realistic situation, which must be considered as the overriding factors. It is not only he who invents something who should be praised, but also he who realizes its potential and employs it effectively!

The French rose to the idea of using a tracked armoured vehicle after their experiments with US Holt agricultural tractors in the towing of artillery. In Great Britain the idea of the tank was put forward as early as October 1914. The first British experiments with the tank only resulted in the armouring of a tractor and this proved unsatisfactory, mainly due to the poor performance across country. The major breakthrough was the suggestion of the rhomboidal shape by (then) Lt.

W. G. Wilson, which enabled the vehicle to cross the high obstacles and wide trenches so characteristic of World War I land warfare. It was due to the requirement for great obstacle clearance that the idea of using a fully rotating turret proved impractical.

The actual events leading to the development of tanks and their eventual use during the Great War is lengthy and forms a subject for further study. Since there is insufficient space here to cover this thoroughly, only the major events are related.

The first experimental tank was ready in January 1916. Two types were eventually built, differing only in their armament. One model (the Male) carried two six-pounder guns, and the

other (the Female) had four machine-guns. When the first tanks were complete, it became of prime importance to conceal their existence from the enemy, and a shroud of secrecy surrounded their manufacture and shipment abroad. For this reason the vehicles were referred to as 'large water tanks for Russia' in all early dispatches. When finally made known to the general public, the word 'tank' caught-on and is still in existence today.

Field Marshal Sir Douglas Haig, commanding the BEF (British Expeditionary Force), authorized the use of tanks in a large-scale attack on the Somme on 15 September 1916. Of the sixty tanks dispatched to France, only thirty-six were suffic-

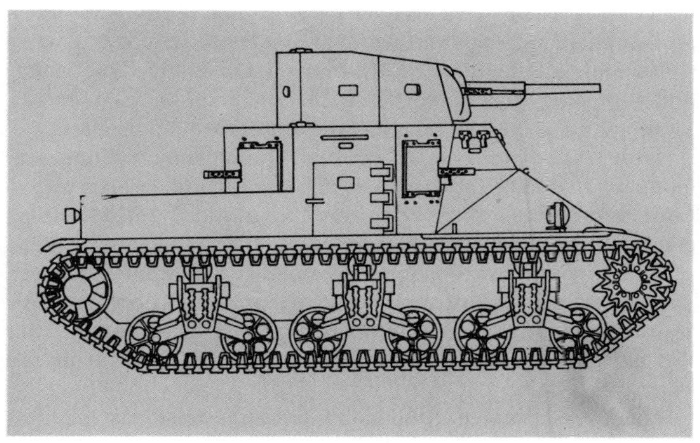

Shown here are three vehicles which, although insignificant in themselves, represented milestones in tank development. (*Left*) the Swedish Strv 33 was a member of a long line of Swedish light tank models which greatly influenced foreign design. (*Above*) the US M2 medium tank, which was later redesigned into the famous M-4 General Sherman. (*Below*) the US Combat Car T-4, utilizing the famous Christie suspension later adopted in British and Russian tank designs.

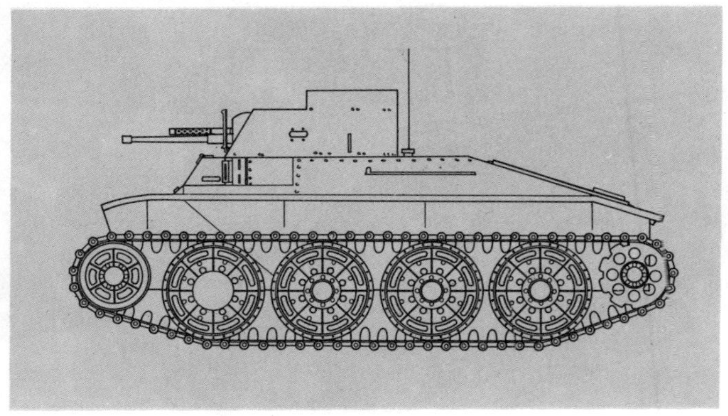

iently reliable to leave the start point. The tanks were used against enemy strong points in widely-spread groups of two or three, and, as a result, achieved only small tactical successes. Following this, Haig requested the production of a further 1,000 which were delivered as slightly improved models.

After experiences of British and French tank actions, the Germans, who probably at that time (for certain, later) realized tank potential to a far greater extent than did the Allies, made efforts to produce their own models. Even so, development of tanks in Germany progressed slowly, and, apart from the production of a handful of their own types and the employment of a slightly larger number of captured Allied models, the Germans never really made any serious use of tanks during the First World War.

The first effective application of tanks took place on 20 November 1917 at Cambrai. The Germans had learnt from

experience that Allied tank attacks were preceded by vast artillery barrages, which not only destroyed any surprise value of this weapon (one of its greatest attributes), but also converted the ground over which the tanks were to advance into a morass of mud, and thereby impaired their mobility. At Cambrai, however, there was no preparatory barrage. Another important factor was that aircraft were used in a ground support role, and a squadron of the Royal Flying Corps was attached to the newly formed Royal Tank Corps. Over 300 tanks advanced across open ground on a frontage of six miles. A breakthrough of the German lines was achieved, which extended to a depth of four miles. This figure was immense compared with the depth of penetration achieved earlier by conventional means (previously a gain of 700 yards was considered a great feat), and was gained without the expense of thousands of lives and tons of expensive artillery ammunition. Infantry losses were minimal, but there were insufficient tanks

Depicted on the left is the Valentine tank, one of the most famous British tanks of the Second World War. Although officially classed as an 'I' (Infantry) tank, it was really a compromise between that and the cruiser type. Its name derived from the fact that the first official War Office orders were placed on St Valentine's Day. This tank was used extensively during the desert campaigns and the initial actions following D-Day. Its chassis was used for a number of self-propelled artillery mountings, one of which (the Archer) remained in service right up until the mid-'fifties.

Opponents in the Western Desert: (*above*) the famous British Matilda II tank; (*below*) the Italian M.11/39. The Matilda II was a true infantry tank, having very thick armour. It was dimensionally very small and mounted only a two-pounder gun. The M.11/39 possessed no really striking attributes but formed one of the major weapons of the Italian Army. The main gun was mounted in the hull front whilst two machine-guns were located in the turret.

available for exploiting the breach, and it was not long before the Germans were able to re-form and halt any further progress. The Cambrai attack had been conceived by the 'Unconventional Soldier', (then) Lt-Col. J. F. C. Fuller. At the Battle of Amiens, on 8 August 1918, a powerful massed tank assault won successes far beyond those of Cambrai. During the final stages of the First World War tanks played a vital part in every action. The use of armour-piercing bullets against tanks was anticipated and later tanks compensated for this by having increased armour. By 1918 the importance of the tank had been really appreciated.

New advocates of the tank arose – making prophecies of

(*Above*) the famous Churchill tank, probably the most successful British tank of the Second World War despite its various shortcomings. It was a heavy infantry tank and, originally, mounted a two-pounder gun in the turret and a three-inch howitzer in the hull. Later models dispensed with the howitzer and had the two-pounder replaced firstly by a six-pounder and later by a 75 mm. This tank was used in Tunisia and later in the Allied landings in Europe. Its chassis was used for a whole host of special purpose vehicles, such as flame-throwers, bridge-layers, mine-sweepers, etc. Even so, only one self-propelled gun version was built and that remained purely experimental. The engineer version (called the AVRE) remained in service right up until the late 'sixties.

future warfare based on the tank and the ideas of General Fuller. Amongst those in Britain, (then) Captain G. Le.Q. Martel was one of the foremost. At a very early date, he wrote: *. . . No present day army could fight against an army consisting of say 2,000 tanks, and it therefore follows that all large continental armies will have to make use of tank armies in the future . . . Tanks will be of such great importance that future great wars are almost sure to start with a duel between the tank armies of separate sides . . .'*

Martel saw the tank also as a weapon to meet and destroy enemy tanks – at a time when combat between tank forces was practically non-existent. Fuller read of Martel's ideas with interest, but he himself put forward far more advanced ideas. In May 1919 he proposed his 'Plan 1919'. Fuller envisaged the tank as a means of executing an entirely new method of land warfare – the avoidance of massed enemy troops and the capture of reserves, HQs, bases, etc. The earlier successes at Cambrai dispelled any protests from the old school (and indeed there were many), and paved the way for further tank opera-

The Crusader tank (*below*) was a direct descendant of the famous American Christie design, and was used extensively during the battles in the Western Desert. It was initially armed with a two-pounder gun but later versions (as shown) had a six-pounder.

(*Above*) the most successful French tank produced before the German occupation, the SOMUA SAU-35. Despite the inheritance of a number of misconceptions extant in earlier tanks, this model caused some concern to the Germans.

being such as to enable close accompaniment of infantry (i.e. very slow). France did, however, maintain a fairly large tank force.

GREAT BRITAIN. The army, in general, paid relatively great attention to the development of armoured fighting vehicles and the manner in which they could be used. Very advanced manoeuvres were held on Salisbury Plain in which some very advanced machines took part. These machines were designed to accomplish the form of warfare advocated by Liddell Hart and Fuller. Their design and development (which was extensive) came under the auspices of the 'War Mechanization Board'. This Board concerned itself with determining what types of vehicles should be adopted by the army, the manner of their use, and how they might be flexibly integrated with the other leading arms. In spite of all this great endeavour, however, the almost financial starvation imposed on the army by the government (in the firm belief that the Great War was the war to end wars) restricted the purchase of any reasonable quantity of these marvellous vehicles with the result that the British Army remained virtually without any form of tank

The remaining two principal tank models used by the French at the beginning of the war: (*below*) the Char B heavy tank; (*right*) the R.35 light tank. Both models were produced in quantity by the Renault firm. The Char B was a remarkable tank from an engineering point of view, although, like all other French tanks, it suffered from misconceptions of armoured warfare. The 75 mm. gun in the hull was aimed by manoeuvring the tank into the required position. To achieve this, a specially designed steering system was incorporated. The turret mounted an effective anti-tank gun, but there was only sufficient room for one man, who was absurdly overworked. The tank was also very slow. The R.35 light tank was a very successful light tank design. It had excellent cast armour, thicker than usual for a light tank, relatively powerful armament, and a fairly high speed. The scissors type suspension, which was very robust, provided the vehicle with a fairly good cross-country performance.

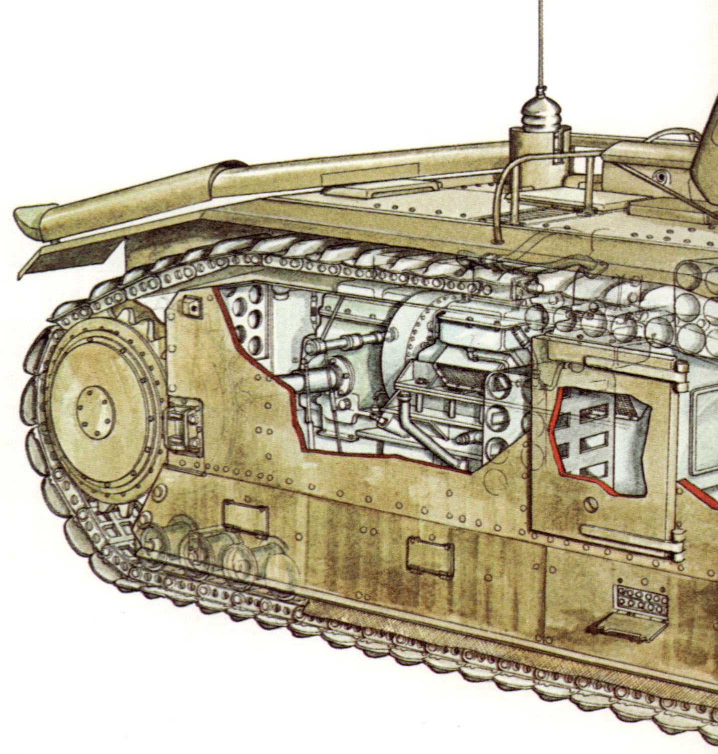

Shown here is the famous Russian T-34/76 tank. This was indisputably the most advanced tank design of its time. It had a profound influence upon all future tank design throughout the Western Hemisphere. In its design the Russians achieved the most effective combination of the requirements of a fighting tank. The 76 mm. gun was a most efficient weapon for that time, and the cleverly sloped thick armour provided the maximum obtainable protection. The Christie suspension and diesel engine were other features worthy of note. High-quality workmanship was only used where considered necessary.

force prior to the gathering of war clouds over Europe.

USA. At this early stage the Americans, like the British, were convinced that there would be no further great wars. For a long time they followed closely the French doctrine of tank warfare.

RUSSIA. Unlike the other European nations at this time, the USSR paid close attention to the development of its tank forces. Russia could not afford an attitude of complacency, since she always considered the possibility of a threat from the non-

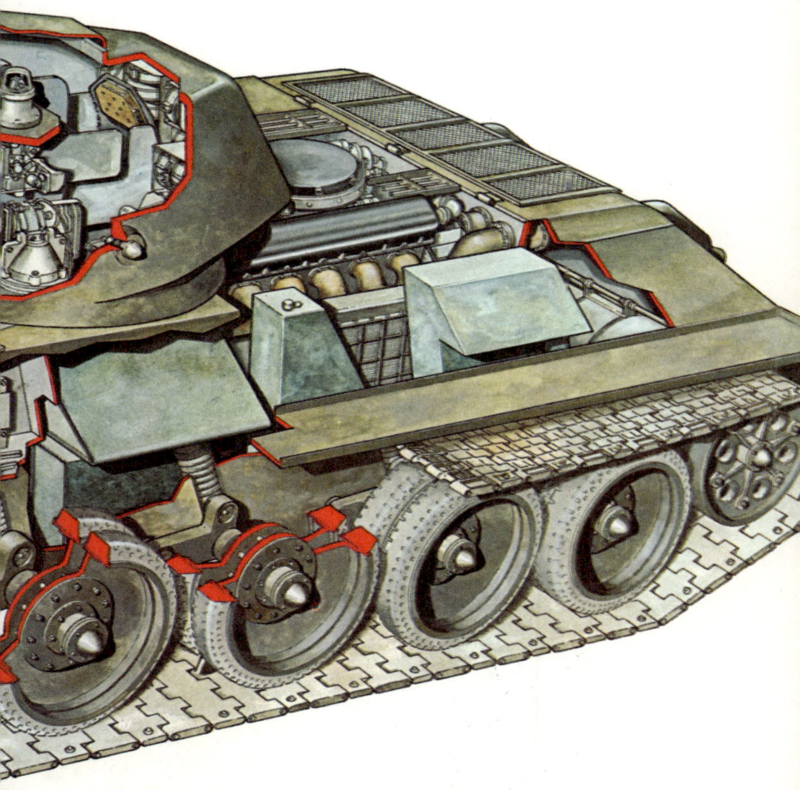

Communist nations in an endeavour to reinstate the previous order. As a result, a very large proportion of government expenditure was allocated to the design and production of arms and the development of new tactics and strategies. Efforts to develop tank models and strategy for their use received a high priority. Initially, the Russians adhered closely to the French doctrines of tank warfare but, with the publication of various books by the English tank prophets and their intelligence regarding the British experiments on Salisbury Plain, they soon adopted a more advanced attitude towards tank employment. The two most notable Soviet tank prophets were Marshal N. Tukhachevsky and Colonel I. V. Kalinovsky. Given a virtually free hand, these officers were able to

(*Below*) the famous Russian KV-1 tank, named after the Soviet War Commissar, Klim Voroshilov. This tank formed the heavy companion to the T-34/76 and mounted the same armament and utilized the same diesel engine and transmission. Despite its great weight, the tank had a fairly high turn of speed and was very manoeuvrable. In the design of the KV the Russians made use of torsion-bar suspension. The model shown has extra armour bolted to the turret.

(*Above*) the Italian L 6/40 light tank. Produced about the same time as the Russian models, one can see how great a lead the Russians had over some countries. This model is a good example of the use of riveted armour construction.

develop a huge tank force in the Soviet Army (by the early 'thirties it numbered over 10,000 armoured fighting vehicles). Three basic means of employing tanks were considered: a) as a means of directly accompanying infantry attacks, b) to be used en masse as a means of penetrating heavily defended positions, and c) for long-range operations against reserves, HQs, etc. in the manner laid down by General Fuller in his 'Plan 1919'.

OTHER COUNTRIES: No other country could, at this time, be considered as a major tank-using nation. The Germans, who fully appreciated the value of tanks, were forbidden from having these, or indeed any other form of strategic weapon, by the terms of the Versailles Treaty. There were, however, a number of technical and tactical developments in some of the smaller countries which contributed greatly to the evolution of armoured warfare. The Swedes and the Czechs both became producers of armoured fighting vehicles and many of their models had a profound influence upon future

Depicted here are the two standard light tank models employed by the Germans at the beginning of World War II. (*Below*) the Pz.Kpfw. II light tank, which was armed with a 20 mm. heavy machine-gun and a lighter 7·62 mm. machine-gun, coaxially mounted in the turret.

(*Above*) the Pz.Kpfw. I light tank. This was originally built as a training tank, but did take part in some early battles of the Second World War. It was only armed with two light machine-guns. Its chassis was later to form the basis of specialised support vehicles.

tank design. The Austrian tank expert, Ludwig Ritter von Eimannsberger wrote many works on tank warfare which could be considered on the level of those by Liddell Hart.

This brings us to 1933, when Hitler came to power in Germany. With the establishment of the Nazi Party in Germany, a considerable amount of money was made available for the expansion of the armaments industry. Hitler rejected the controls upon German rearmament laid down in the Versailles Treaty and gave great encouragement to the production of weapons. As regards tanks (and indeed other arms forbidden under the terms of the Versailles Treaty), Germany was not so far behind other nations as was thought. During the late 'twenties and early 'thirties, Hans Seekt, (then) Commander-in-Chief of the German Army, had satisfactorily negotiated a rapprochement with the Soviets by which secret German experimental and training establishments were established in Western Russia. By this means the Germans were able to develop new weapons and techniques of warfare without the knowledge of the Entente. From the Russian point of view, it was a means of acquiring all the modern technologies and manufacturing processes gained by the long-established German military-industrial complex.

The Germans were, therefore, by the mid-'thirties in possession of a formidable armed force (Wehrmacht). The newly appointed commander of the German armoured and motorized troops (called fast troops) was Colonel (later General) Heinz Guderian. Guderian, as mentioned earlier, had made a detailed analytical study of the writings of Liddell Hart and orientated his new tactical conceptions of mechanized warfare around these. It became necessary to test these ideas – even though they had been substantiated by the results of war-games and exercises. An opportunity presented itself with the outbreak of the Spanish Civil War. The Germans supported the Fascist troops by providing German armoured vehicles, artillery and aircraft. These were often manned by German personnel.

Towards the end of the war, the effectiveness of the light tank declined. The only nation to continue development of the light tank for its original function (i.e. as a fighting tank) was the United States. Shown above is the US M-24 General Chaffee light tank, which mounted a light-weight, but potent, 75 mm. anti-tank gun. This vehicle appeared towards the end of 1944 and took part in the battles from then on. It continued in service after the war up until the mid-'fifties, but by this time it had been relegated to use as a reconnaissance vehicle. It still continues to be used by other nations even today, and has been employed by the South Vietnamese.

(*Below*) the final production model of the German light tank of World War II: the Lynx. As with most other countries at this time, the Germans employed light tanks as reconnaissance vehicles and when first encountered by Allied Intelligence in official German reports some confusion was caused through the German nomenclature. The Germans designated the vehicle as a *Panzerspähwagen*, which was the term previously applied to wheeled armoured reconnaissance vehicles. This clearly demonstrated the entirely new attitude being taken towards light tanks. The Lynx was an extremely good design and utilized the over-lapping bogie wheel suspension system so often encountered on heavier German tank models. It was armed with a 20 mm. heavy machine-gun.

It is rather ironic, in retrospect, that the Russians supported the other side (the Republicans) in exactly the same way, although there was no direct confrontation between German and Soviet troops. It is also interesting that the Germans and the Russians came to completely opposite conclusions as to the manner in which tanks should be employed, following their individual analyses of this conflict.

The application of tanks and aircraft by the Germans in the Spanish Civil War allowed them to develop the new Panzer Division, an entirely new concept in military organization and tactics. Where the French had discarded the idea of fast tanks

The Pz.Kpfw.III was the standard German medium tank at the start of the war. It saw action in practically every German armoured battle of the war. It was most often armed with a long-barrelled 50 mm. anti-tank gun.

on the grounds that they would lose contact with the other slower-moving arms, the Germans came to the rather obvious conclusion that – rather than slow the tanks down to their speeds – why not put everyone else on wheels so that they can keep up with the tanks?

The Panzer Division, therefore, was a special type of division which was composed of various members and equipments from all arms (the Tank Corps, Infantry, Artillery, Ordnance etc), mounted on armoured or semi-armoured vehicles, and capable of fighting as one separate body. Placing all these now mobile armoured equipments under the jurisdiction of one divisional commander allowed greater flexibility of control, faster reaction to particular events, and greater concentration of firepower at any particular point.

Since, by virtue of its concept of mobility, the Panzer Division was designed to operate in open flat terrain (i.e. avoid areas where vehicles could be ambushed and which would slow down the momentum of the attack), a further, second type of division was required for close country. This division was called the Panzergrenadier Division (Armoured Infantry Division). The difference between these two divisions was primarily the mix of vehicles. Where the Panzer Division was composed primarily of tanks and armoured cars, with a smaller complement of armoured infantry carriers (half-tracks), the Panzergrenadier Division was vice versa. Thus, in a manner, the new German organization of their fighting troops had reverted to the old form of medieval times. The knight-in-armour was the Panzer unit, the infantryman the Panzer-grenadier unit.

The effectiveness of the new German organization was to be demonstrated with the initial phases of the Second World War.

In the meantime, the only other nation with a sizeable tank force, the USSR, was also carrying out drastic reorganizational changes, but, in this case, with negative results. The Russian tank experts, Tukhachevsky and Kalinovsky, had built up a vast tank arm on rather similar lines to that of Germany – the main difference being that breakthroughs were to be achieved by a series of blows rather than one aimed thrust. As mentioned earlier, special tank units had been formed in order to achieve this.

During the mid-'thirties, Stalin decided to purge the Army of so-called 'reactionaries'. In reality it was an action to destroy any possible competitors to his position. Needless to say, Tukhachevsky and Kalinovsky were strongly criticized for their almost disciple-like adherence to the theories of Fuller and Liddell Hart and, what with these and various other rather

The Pz.Kpfw.IV was originally designed as a medium support tank and mounted a short 75 mm. howitzer. The need for more powerfully armed medium tanks, however, necessitated its continual up-gunning. The vehicle shown below mounted a long-barrelled 75 mm. anti-tank gun.

The most advanced German medium tank of the war was the Panther. The design of this tank was orientated around that of the famous Russian T-34, although many peculiarly German features were incorporated, such as the overlapping suspension.

obscure and complicated charges, they were eventually executed. Command of the Soviet tank forces now came under the jurisdiction of General Pavlov, who commanded the Soviet tank forces in the Spanish Civil War. Drawing erroneous conclusions from this war, it was decided that massed tank attacks were unnecessary and wasteful and that the most efficient manner in which to use tanks was that adopted by the French. The result was the breaking down of the special tank units into packets of tanks for distribution to infantry formations.

Virtually no other development in tank technology or tactics took place before the German occupation of Czechoslovakia. It was about this time that the British Government began to realize that there might well be another war and that they ought to make some effort to provide the army with tanks. Although there had been a great deal of progress earlier with the Experimental Mechanized Force on Salisbury Plain, things had become rather out of date. The current medium tank model of the British army up until 1937 was a model which had been produced during 1926! In addition, the High Command was not completely convinced of the validity of the Panzer Division concept.

Two entirely different approaches to tank design were ultimately followed by the British (the light tank model is excluded): there was one trend towards an 'I' (Infantry) model for application in a similar manner to the French, and the other towards a 'Cavalry' tank to be used in a similar manner to the German Panzers. This policy continued almost until the end of the war. The 'I' tank was a relatively slow vehicle with very thick armour and machine-gun armament, although later on this was replaced by an anti-tank gun. The Cruiser model was a fast tank with relatively light armour and an anti-tank gun (there were special models with howitzers for firing H.E.).

The Second World War became the War of Mechanization. The effect of the Second World War upon the development of armoured fighting vehicles is a complex subject to analyze. Basically, the subject may be split into two parts: a) technological development, and b) tactical development.

I think it is fair to say that practically all technological development stemmed from the actions on the Eastern Front. When the Germans launched their 'Operation Barbarossa' against Russia, on 22 June 1941, they were under the impression that current Soviet tank models were technically inferior

Perhaps the most famous and most spectacular tank of the war was the German 'Tiger', shown below. This heavy tank was designed for the Russian Front, although it saw action in the desert and Western Europe. It mounted the deadly German 88 mm. gun.

to their own. In reality, the Russians had developed two tank models – the T–34 medium and the KV heavy – which were a generation in advance of their time. The medium model had thick sloping armour making it almost immune to any existing anti-tank guns, a very powerful high-velocity 76 mm. anti-tank gun, and a very robust diesel engine providing minimal fire-risk, long-range and high power-to-weight ratio. It also used a modified form of the US Christie suspension which facilitated high speeds across country. The heavy KV model, on the other hand, had very thick armour all round, a reasonable speed, the same high-power diesel engine and the same armament. The suspension was a torsion-bar type which proved more suitable for such a heavy type tank. Production

Towards the end of the war, the German Royal Tiger appeared, which had much thicker armour and a more powerful gun. The concrete-like appearance of the surface was created by the application of a special paste to counter magnetic and sticky mines.

of these two vehicles was begun very shortly before the German attack, with the result that only some 1,500 were in service at that time. Even so, their effects upon the German armoured troops were phenomenal.

During their previous campaigns in France and Western Europe, as well as the campaign currently taking place in the Western Desert, the Germans had rarely met any form of armour which proved superior to their own. Only two models caused any anxiety – the French SOMUA SAU–35 and the British Matilda Infantry Tank Mk. II. Both these tanks were found in only relatively small numbers, however, with the result that their overall effects were minimal. The British model had extremely thick armour (up to 88 mm.), but was armed with a relatively small gun (the two-pounder), and in the desert actions it was found necessary to run the gauntlet of enemy fire before any retaliatory shots could be made.

If the Russians had not discarded the mobile-war concepts

This cut-away drawing shows the interior of the US Stuart light tank, a vehicle supplied to almost all Allied armies through Lend-Lease. It is typical of the layout of all light tanks, and indeed American tanks in general. Of particular interest are the anti-aircraft machine-gun and the tractor-like suspension.

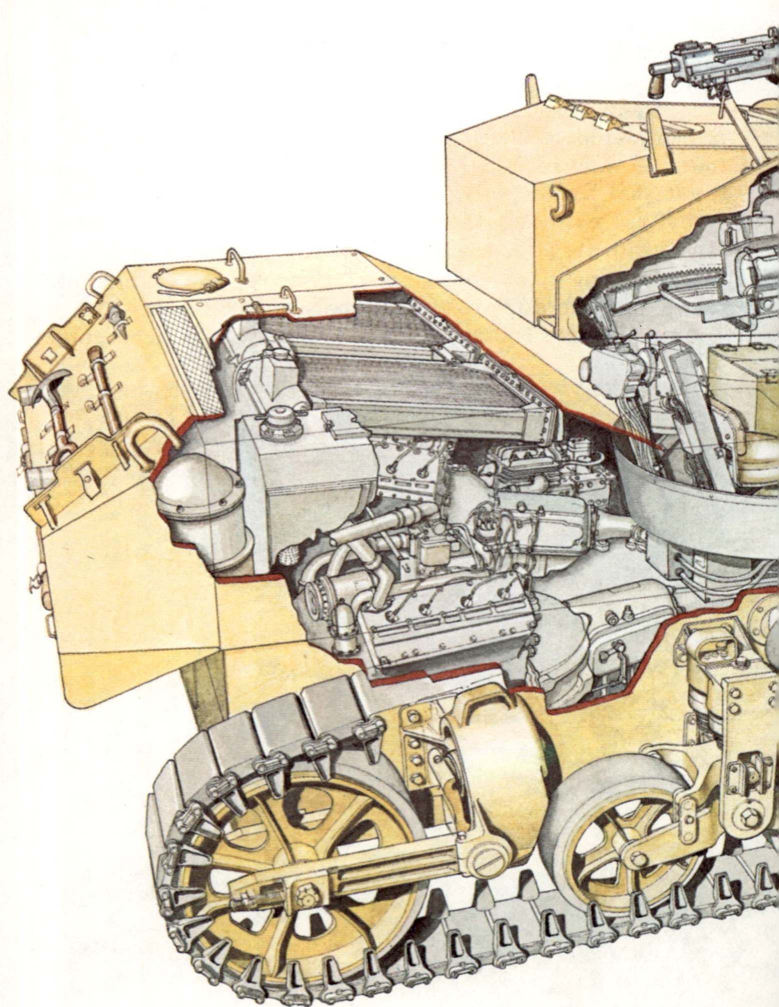

introduced by Tukhachevsky and Kalinovsky, then perhaps they might have stemmed the German advances at a much earlier date. As it was, a very large proportion of their tanks were obsolete or in a poor state of repair and those new models (T–34 and KV) which they possessed were spread too thinly

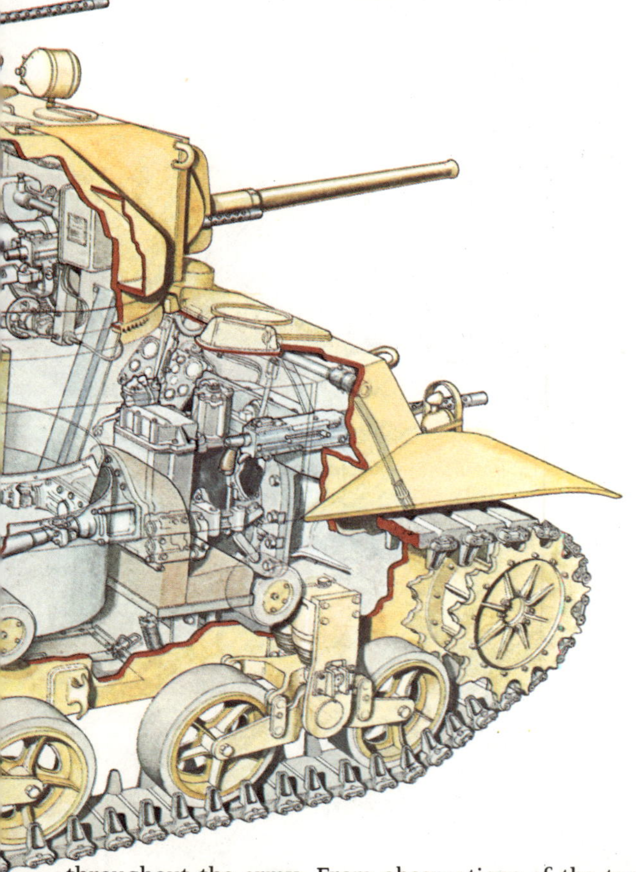

throughout the army. From observations of the tank battles taking place in Western Europe, the Russians made great efforts to reform their tank units into the mechanized form adopted prior to the Spanish Civil War. When the Germans

Prior to the manufacture of the Sherman tank, the Americans produced the famous General Grant M-3 tank (*above*), which saw action in the Western desert. A 75 mm. gun was mounted in the right sponson.

attacked, however, everything was in a state of flux and very few mechanized units had been formed. On the other hand, the earlier purges of the officer corps had seriously weakened Soviet leadership and there was a great shortage of experienced and talented commanders. The Germans, despite numerical inferiority and their initial shock in meeting such remarkable Soviet tanks, employed their new Panzer divisions and 'thrust tactics' with the utmost skill. As a result, they defeated over 17,500 Soviet tanks within the first six months of the Soviet-German campaign. They also captured a major proportion of Soviet fighting troops and the principal tank and automotive plants.

However, the Russians had catered for defence needs in a most skilful way. Many of their large tank plants had been established in the Eastern districts such as the Urals, which were

Final Allied medium tank development of World War II. (*Left*) the US General Pershing M-26 tank, which mounted a deadly 90 mm. gun and had very thick cast armour. Torsion-bar suspension was used. (*Above*) the British Centurion, which arrived in service just too late to take part in operations. It was certainly the most advanced tank in the world for its time, and was a complete departure from previous British tank designs. The model shown is a later version with a twenty-pounder gun which has the characteristic British bore-evacuator midway along the barrel. This was to enable the clearance of fumes from the barrel.

Final model of the Soviet T-34 medium tank: the T-34/85. This was a modification of the original model, but having a new turret mounting an 85 mm. dual-purpose gun. This model remained in service for many years and saw action in Korea.

not only well out of reach of any possible immediate German advances, but were also fairly safe from German bombers. As soon as the Russians realized that their Western tank plants were to be overrun, they evacuated them completely to these Eastern districts where they were formed into 'Tank Cities'. Three such cities were formed – the two most prominent being Uralmashzavod and Tankograd. The former produced nothing but T–34s and special vehicles based on the T–34, while the latter built nothing but KVs and their derivatives.

The tremendous influx of superior Russian tanks forced the Germans to develop models of their own which could fight on equal, or better, terms. Two new German tanks appeared – the medium Panther (which was as near a copy of the Russian T–34 as the Germans could conveniently make) with its

long-barrelled 75 mm. gun, and the heavy Tiger with its 88 mm. gun. The existing models of the current medium tanks Pz.Kpfw. III and IV were also up-armoured and up-gunned.

As soon as production of these new German models got fully underway, the new tanks began to appear in units of the German Afrika Korps under the command of Erwin Rommel.

Both the British and the Russians could not, at that time, compete with German production potential, or so they thought. (It was a common error at that time to over-estimate the quantities of German tanks – a tendency resulting from the enormous impact that they had caused.) By this time the United States had been brought into the war, and with it appeared the enormous American military industrial complex. Through a military-political agreement termed 'Lend-Lease', the United States provided both Britain and Russia with enormous numbers of vehicles. Canada, too, took part in this programme. From the Russian point of view, their needs were not so much for armoured fighting vehicles but for military lorries and cars. These were necessary to provide some

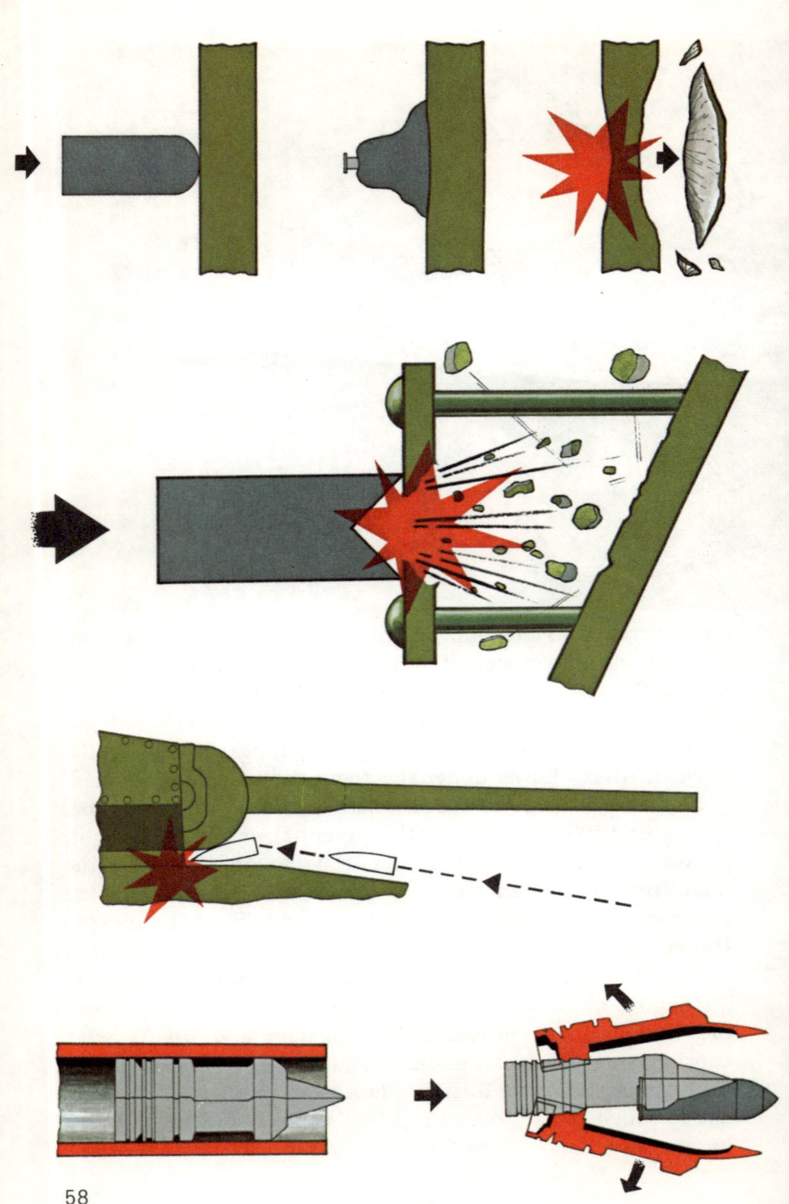

reasonable logistical tail to their front-line troops. Indeed, most of the American tanks provided at that time were significantly inferior to the Russian models, although they did possess a number of technical sophistications, and were used mainly to defend the Eastern regions from attack by Japan.

Supply of American vehicles to Britain, however, was of the greatest significance. Britain had lost almost her entire stock of armoured vehicles at Dunkirk in 1940, and her industry was unable to turn out sufficient quantities of tanks under the best conditions. Initially, the Americans provided the famous M–3 (General Grant) tank, which had a sponson-mounted 75 mm. gun and a turret-mounted 37 mm. anti-tank gun. The 37 mm. gun was used as an anti-tank weapon but since it was of too small a calibre to fire high-explosive, the 75 mm. gun performed this role. The Grant tank proved its worth in the fighting in the Western Desert, but the limited traverse of the 75 mm. gun was found to be a serious handicap. A new design then appeared, the M–4 General Sherman, which retained almost the same hull and suspension as the M–3, but now had the 75 mm. gun mounted in a larger, fully-rotating turret. This gun, for the first time, could fire both armour-piercing and high-explosive ammunition. The Sherman tank proved so successful that it remained the most dominant Allied tank until the end of the war. It did, however, undergo a number of modifications.

(*Left*) methods of penetrating tank armour. (*Top*) the HESH (High-Explosive Squash Head), also referred to as HEP (High-Explosive Plastic). This round distorts on impact to increase the area of contact between explosive and plate. The special plastic explosive transmits a shock-wave through the armour which releases a 'scab' from the inside surface, rather on the lines of 'Newton's Cradle'. (*Centre*) the effect of the hollow-charge against armour and a method of countering it. A concave parabolic reflector reflects a parallel plasma of molten explosive towards the armour which is sufficiently concentrated to drill a hole. A commonly-used counter-measure is the 'spaced-plate' which causes detonation of the round before impact with the main armour. The lower illustration shows the effect of shell-traps, and, (*bottom*) the mechanism of the discarding sabot.

With the appearance of the new German tank models – the Panther and the Tiger – both the Russians and the Western Allies turned out improved vehicles to counteract them. The Russians up-gunned the T–34 with a new turret mounting an 85 mm. gun, and completely redesigned the KV tank into the Iosef Stalin, initially mounting an 85 mm. gun but finally a 122 mm. gun. The Americans produced the new Sherman model mounting the 76 mm. anti-tank gun, whilst the British re-armed the Sherman with their new potent seventeen-pounder anti-tank gun.

Although the British made full use of the American models, they did produce a number of tanks of their own. All British tanks of the Second World War received an 'A' number. The Infantry series was comprised of three models – the Matilda (A–12), mentioned earlier, the Valentine (A–10) and the Churchill (A–22). The medium (or Cruiser models) started with the A–13, the Crusader (A–15), and progressed through the Cavalier, Centaur, Cromwell and Comet. The famous Centurion (A–41) did not appear in time to go into action.

The Americans experimented with numerous heavy tanks

(*Above*) the latest British Chieftain tank with its deadly 120 mm. gun. This gun fires both HESH and APDS ammunition.
(*Left*) the Vickers light tank, which was built as a private venture for sales abroad. It was used by the Indians during the recent Indo-Pakistan war. The main armament is a 105 mm. gun, but the armour is extremely thin for a tank of this size. (*Below*) the latest variant of the Centurion tank, which is in service with several NATO armies. This mounts a 105 mm. gun and is fitted with infra-red night driving and fighting equipment. In the British Army it is being replaced by Chieftain.

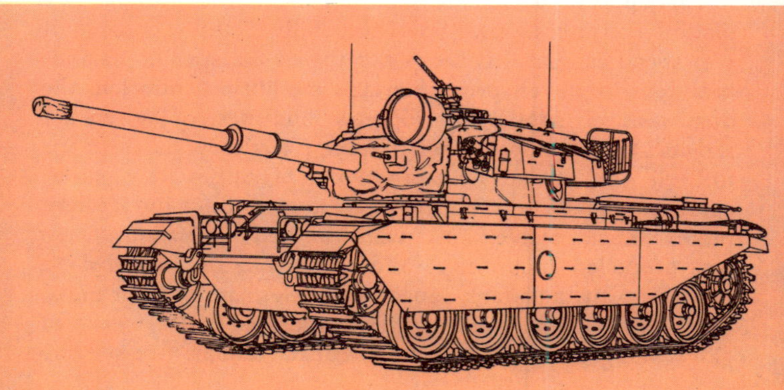

(*Below*) the French AMX-13 light tank. This was a revolutionary French light tank design produced during the early 'fifties, but is still to be found in service with many armies today. It was the first service tank to make use of the oscillating turret concept enabling the mounting of very powerful guns in relatively light vehicles. Special provisions have been made to enable this vehicle to fire modern anti-tank missiles, such as the SS-11, Entac, Milan and HOT. These have been achieved without detriment to the normal capabilities of the tank. One of its greatest attributes is its ease of airportability. The French have standardized a whole series of special support vehicles on this chassis, such as AA tanks, armoured personnel carriers, self-propelled guns, engineer vehicles and bridge-layers.

but the first to enter service, the M–26 Pershing, saw very little action. They preferred to rely heavily on the well-proven M–4 Sherman and a fleet of tank-destroyers.

The appearance of the tank-destroyer was inspired by tactical considerations. When originally defining a tank, it was specified that this weapon satisfied the specific balance between firepower, protection and mobility. It also had the dual task of supporting infantry and destroying enemy armour. With the occupation of foreign territory, the Germans utilized the native tank-production facilities to convert captured chassis into limited-traverse mountings for artillery pieces. Such conversions were termed *Selbstfahrlafetten* (self-propelled mountings) and were initially intended to bolster-up the anti-tank capability of German artillery units. The German artillery arm, rather disgruntled by the wealth of glory being bestowed upon the Panzer troops, pressed the

High Command for its own special armoured fighting vehicles. The result was that a large proportion of German production chassis were turned over to use for self-propelled guns. Practically all of these mountings were limited-traverse. Towards the end of the war, there was a whole range of special artillery vehicles under development, and these were referred to as *Einheitswaffenträger* (standard weapons carriers).

In other armies the adoption of self-propelled weapons was more realistic. The Soviets developed a range of vehicles based on the T–34 and KV chassis to mount limited-traverse artillery weapons, and these became known as SU or SAU *(Samochodno-Artilleriyskie-Ustanovki* = Self-Propelled Artillery Mounting). The Russians also produced a wide range of self-

(*Above*) the latest French main battle tank AMX-30. This tank reflects current French attitudes to tank design. Although, from an engineering standpoint, a very well-designed tank, it incorporates certain trends which cause much controversy. The armour is extremely thin (being no more than one would expect on a modern light tank), and the armament has several disadvantages. The calibre of 105 mm. is inadequate for a tank of this size and the sophisticated hollow-charge round fired by this gun involves the use of complicated and time-consuming sighting devices. The road and cross-country performances, however, are excellent and the tank incorporates the most up-to-date aids for night-fighting, gas and radiation proofing, and river crossing. The chassis is being utilized for a large range of special armoured support vehicles.

Shown below is the revolutionary Swedish S-tank which, as a result of the rigid mounting of the 105 mm. gun in the hull and the hydro-pneumatic suspension, is extremely low and difficult to hit.

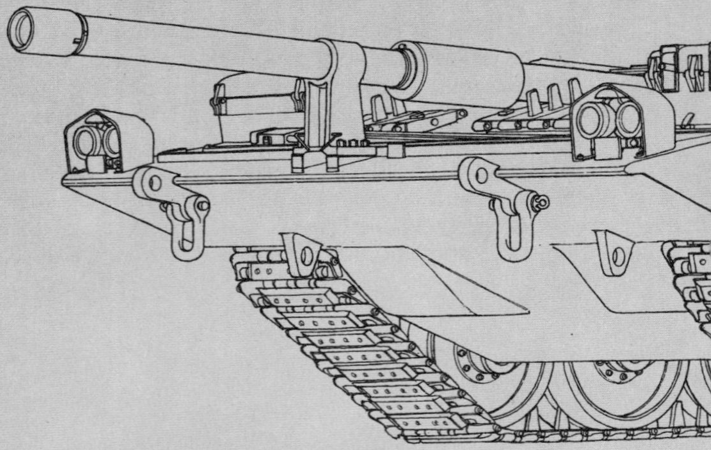

The Japanese Type 61 medium tank. During the Second World War, the Japanese developed their tanks especially for fighting in the Pacific, i.e. light, fast and small. These tanks could traverse areas normally unnegotiable by foreign tanks. Post-war Japanese tank design, however, reflects trends extant in European tanks and caters for the peculiar requirements of the Japanese Self-Defence Force. The Japanese are currently experimenting with the ST-B medium tank which is a most exceptional vehicle with many new features.

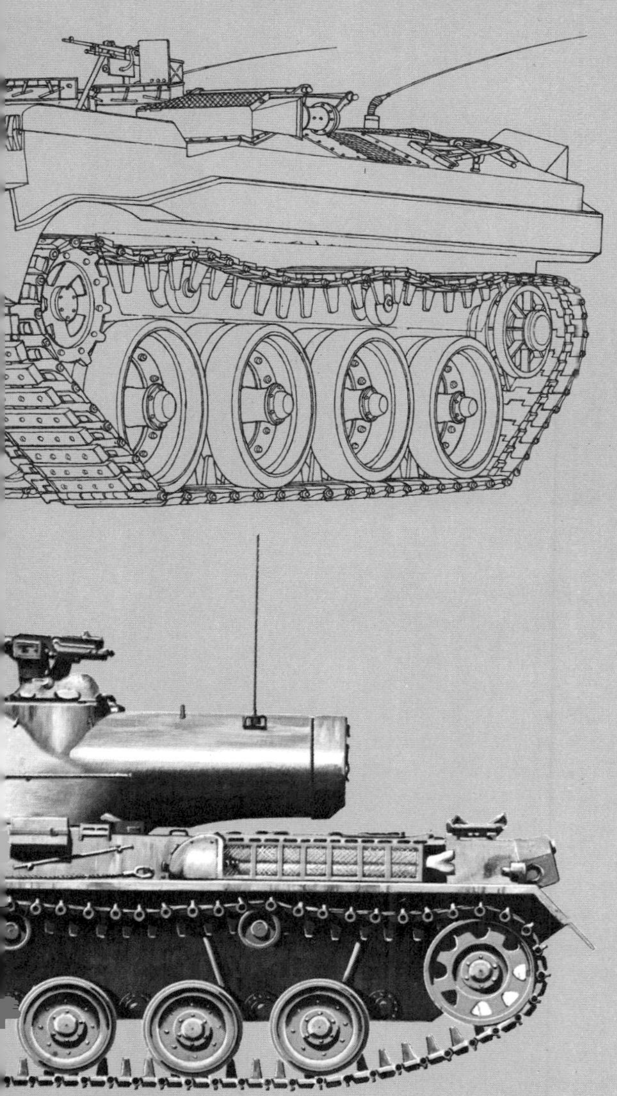

The German Leopard tank has been a most successful design and is being supplied to several armies apart from the West German. Designed along similar lines to the French AMX-30 it is, however, a much more effective and lethal tank.

propelled rocket-launchers based on both wheeled and tracked vehicles.

In the case of the British and Americans, however, the demand for self-propelled artillery was more acute. Here, the need was for self-propelled anti-tank guns suitable for the engagement of the new German armour. Apart from using American versions, the British produced their own models.

The Americans introduced the M–10 and M–36 tank destroyers which, unlike other models, had fully rotating turrets. These were, however, originally open on top. The introduction of these vehicles made the distinction between tank and self-propelled gun extremely subtle; their resemblance to a conventional tank was exceptionally close. It was, however, their role which distinguished them from tanks, in that their sole task was the seeking out and engagement of enemy armour. No considerations were given to the support of infantry or the assault of heavily-defended positions. Towards the end of the war, the British also brought out a number of free-traverse turreted mountings for the seventeen-pounder gun (Avenger and Challenger), but these were not widely used.

Despite the great need for self-propelled anti-tank guns, the British and Americans utilized their standard chassis for limited-traverse artillery mountings. The Sherman chassis was employed as a gun-motor-carriage for the 105 mm. howitzer (M–7 Priest), the 155 mm. howitzer (M–12), and the 8 in. howitzer (M–43). In the war against Japan the Americans also used a number of super-heavy self-propelled mountings having weapons up to 240 mm. calibre!

Very little has been said about the light tank. This is because the part played by light tanks proved relatively insignificant. Interestingly enough, the light tank was one of the most numerically dominant models at the start of the war and a very large proportion of tanks of all armies were light models. The appearance of effective anti-tank guns, however, made it virtually impossible to provide such a vehicle with any minimal degree of immunity and hence it gradually disappeared from service. One or two countries did continue to use the light tank, however, but under restricted conditions. To the Germans its main value was as a 'tracked armoured

The US M-60 tank is the standard medium tank of the American Army and, to a lesser extent than the Leopard, has been supplied to other armies. It has few particularly noteworthy points.

car' – providing a means of reconnaissance and communication for the all-tracked Panzer and Panzergrenadier divisions. In the American and British armies the light tank provided a means of increasing the offensive power of airborne units, and both the M–22 Locust (American) and the Tetrarch (British) took part in various airborne operations of the Second World War. The Russians, on the other hand, lost faith completely in this type of vehicle and turned all production facilities over to the conversion of existing vehicles to self-propelled field artillery mountings, such as the SU–76.

As far as the tank was concerned, the gradual increase in anti-tank capability (particularly with the introduction of the sub-calibre round and the shaped-charge) caused the adoption of heavier armour and increases in size and weight. Towards the end of the war the Germans had two super-heavy tank projects under construction (the Maus and the E–100) which were to weigh about 150 tons and mount guns ranging from 128 mm. to 170 mm. The British were working on a super-heavy anti-tank SP called the Tortoise which mounted a thirty-two-pounder gun, and the Americans on the T–95 tank which mounted a long-barrelled, high-velocity 105 mm. gun in a limited traverse mount. The Russians, on the other hand, used great skill and ingenuity to redesign their KV model into the IS–III, or Iosef Stalin – which, in spite of a 122 mm. gun and very thick armour, still weighed less than any other existing tank of this type. In this design the Russians managed to achieve extra protection by the use of special shaped-

(*Above left*) the latest Soviet medium tank, the T-62. This vehicle is a more sophisticated redesign of the earlier T-54 and mounts an effective 115 mm. anti-tank gun. Like most Russian tanks it has factory-fitted infra-red night-fighting and driving equipment and deep-wading equipment. It was not intended to replace the T-54/T-55 series but merely to act as a booster to the anti-tank capability of Soviet armoured units. (*Above*) the British Scorpion light tank, in this case with a 76 mm. gun. Another version mounts the very effective Rarden heavy machine-gun which is capable of penetrating the armour of all vehicles, with the exclusion of the heaviest tanks. Note the undercut turret which produces the hazard depicted on page 58. (*Below*) the new joint American/German MBT (Main Battle Tank) 70 represents the ultimate in present-day technological sophistication. It utilizes hydro-pneumatic suspension, the 155 mm. shillelagh missile launcher, laser-range-finder, a very powerful engine, and many more advanced features. The location of the driver in the turret reduces the height to a minimum.

castings, faceted armour and low tank height. Their approach to the problem of heavy tank design revolutionized post-war tank design throughout the Western hemisphere.

Apart from super-heavy tanks, the Germans developed heavy chassis to carry enormous siege guns. One model, the Mrs Karl 040, weighed 123 tons, was over 30 feet long and mounted either a 54 cm. or a 60 cm. mortar (both interchangeable). A few of these weapons were used during the siege of Sevastopol. One of the most ambitious German projects was the transportation system for the huge K–5 gun, which consisted of slinging the gun between two Tiger tank chassis.

By the time the war had come to an end, all armies were practically unanimous over two points:

Tank suspension systems are of great importance; the British Horstmann system, used on the Conqueror and Chieftain, is shown below. Everything concerned with the suspension system is visible in the illustration, demonstrating how little room is taken up inside the tank hull.

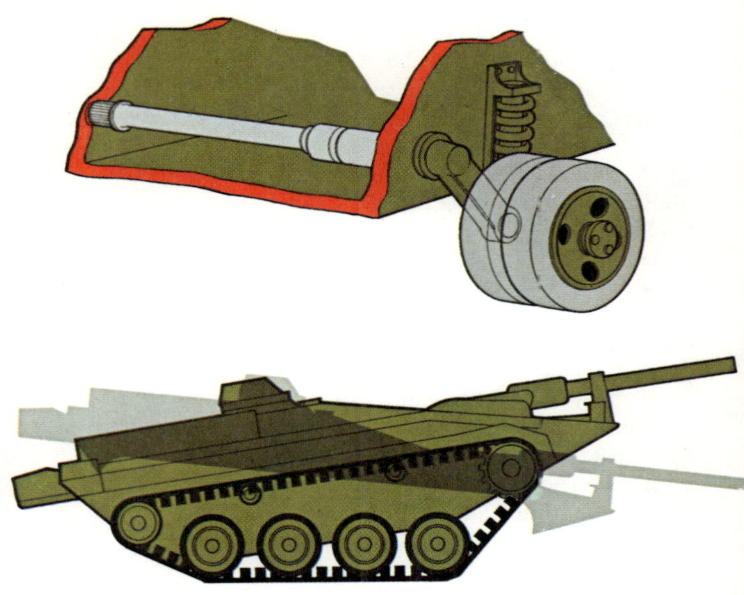

The torsion-bar type suspension (*top*) showing how it necessitates room inside the tank and the subsequent difficulty of access. The lower illustration demonstrates how the hydro-pneumatic suspension on the S-tank facilitates elevation of the gun.

a) that only the medium tank model was operationally useful;
b) that a high degree of standardization was required in future models.

As regards the value of the medium tank, the US had found the Sherman to be extremely useful, while the British favoured their seventeen-pounder gun tanks, the Russians their T–34, and the Germans their Panther.

The mere existence of the Russian IS–III, however, created a need amongst post-war NATO armies for a heavy tank which could fight it on equal terms, but more will be said about this later on.

As regards standardization, the Americans had achieved

this to a remarkable degree; they had fought almost the entire war with only two basic tank models – the M–3 light (and its derivative the M–5) and the M–4 Sherman medium. All their specialized vehicles, such as self-propelled guns, ammunition carriers, etc., were based on the chassis of these two tanks. A similar state of affairs existed in the Soviet Army; the T–34 and KV tanks lasted out the war, although the T–34 underwent minor redesign and the KV was extensively modified to form the Stalin.

In the case of the British and the Germans, however, the situation was different. The British had no less than six tank models in production at any one time, and development from one model to the other was rapid and extensive. Even so, the predominance of US vehicles provided under the Lend-Lease Agreement tended to swamp this fact into insignificance. The Germans, however, mostly as a result of their experiences with Russian tanks, were in a similar situation to the British, but with one major difference – there was no major industrial ally such as the United States to rely upon.

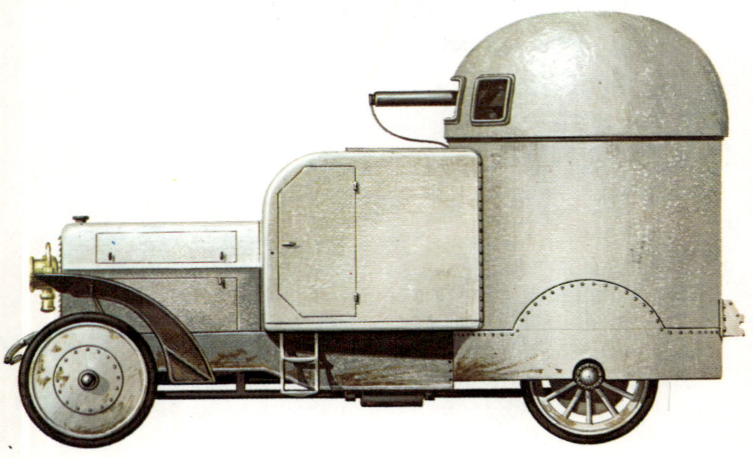

The Austro-Daimler was one of the first armoured cars to be placed in production. It entered service during 1903. The armament consisted of one 37 mm. gun and one or two machine-guns, mounted in a fully-rotating armoured turret.

The need for development and redesign occurred at such a pace that German production was hard-pressed to keep up. Even though German designers and manufacturers managed to keep abreast of tactical requirements, everything had to be hurried, with the inevitable result that reliability suffered. Teething troubles plagued the German Panzer divisions right from the very start, and no German tank ever proved as mechanically reliable as the Russian and American models. The most reliable model in German use was the Czech Pz.38T vehicle, produced by the Praga factory in Czechoslovakia. It was the existence of this tank and the huge military-industrial capability of Czechoslovakia which added extra weight to Hitler's decision to overrun Czechoslovakia. The relatively large numbers of Pz.38 and its companion Czech tank, the Pz.35T, helped to boost the fighting strength of the then weakly-armed Panzer divisions during the Battle of France. The reliability and remarkable characteristics of the Pz.38T were such that, even as late as 1944/45, it was still considered to be a leading design. Its low production cost, good perform-

The Peerless armoured car was, together with the Austin (a very similar vehicle), a standard British armoured car of World War I. The juxtaposition of the turrets was a novel feature. The vehicle entered service during 1917.

ance and high mechanical reliability were such that all German tank production (with the exception of the heavy models) was to be based on this tank.

The main cause for concern over German designs, at least from the point of view of the Western Allies, was their superiority in firepower and armour protection. The German tanks were so heavily armed and armoured that British and American models proved virtually defenceless against them. During the hard fighting following D-Day, the conflict between German and Allied armour proved to be highly significant. Prior to the introduction of the seventeen-pounder and high-

velocity 76 mm. gun, it was virtually impossible to pierce the armour of the German Tiger. These tanks did not even bother to hide; they just sat in the open waiting for Allied armour to appear. Frequently a Sherman would fire several rounds at a Tiger and, after watching these ricochet left and right, would sit there at the mercy of the deadly 88 mm. gun. As soon as the new Allied guns appeared, the situation changed dramatically, and a duel between tanks became as skilful and cunning as a sword fight. One hit upon any tank spelt death. The ultimate criterion became the unleashing of the first round with high accuracy. This was the stage to which tanks had progressed by the end of the Second World War.

There was one other development towards the end of the war which was of great significance to the future development of armour; the invention of the Atomic Bomb.

After 1945 the victorious armies paused to contemplate the enormous quantity of factual statistics gained during the war, together with the influence of atomic weapons upon armies in general, which required deep analysis. Initially, a great deal of speculation was made over the very use of tanks. The ease

One of the most famous armoured cars of World War I was the Rolls Royce, which was also used to a large extent during the desert actions of the Second World War. A special armoured body with a fully-rotating turret was fitted to a modified Rolls-Royce passenger-car chassis. The armament usually consisted of a water-cooled Vickers machine-gun. The vehicles used during the First World War quite often had solid tyres. The car has special significance in that it has been personally employed by many well-known military figures.

with which tanks could be defeated by one aimed round, or by a shaped-charge, and the destructive potential of nuclear weapons, seriously threatened the security of the tank. The idea seemed to prevail that the tank was at long last 'vulnerable'. The reputation which this weapon had gained over the years was one of a huge, slow-moving, iron monster, having absolute immunity to any form of attack. This false conception of the tank was born out of ignorance and exaggerated statements by journalists and romantics. The tank has never enjoyed a period of complete immunity; it was never intended to be impregnable. The tank was designed purely to allow a relatively safe passage during an attack, and to provide protection from all *the most likely* weapons available to the enemy. By restricting the number of weapons which can effectively engage and destroy a tank, it becomes fairly improbable that an enemy has the capability at any specific point to destroy more than a certain number of tanks. It has been mentioned earlier, that during the first six months of the

(*Below*) the Italian Ansaldo armoured car produced during 1915. An interesting feature of this vehicle was the arrangement of the armament, which is apparent from the illustration. This armoured car was used by a number of countries.

war, the Russians lost 17,500 tanks; this represents an enormous number. Yet, did they discard this weapon as impractical and tactically useless? They did not; in fact their appreciation of the value of the tank became more apparent. For as long as the tank continues to be the safest, fastest, most efficient and most cost-effective weapon system capable of gaining ground, its future is assured. (The cost of producing, manning and running ten modern battle tanks is less than that required for one tactical fighter!)

It was the war in Korea which finally put an end to any pessimistic view of tank warfare. The tank in Korea showed that, under modern warfare conditions, such a vehicle was still the most economic means of winning a land battle. Even though nuclear weapons were not used in this conflict or any since (pray they never will be!), it was considered that the tank was of even greater value than before. One of the best cases for the value of tanks in future war was that put forward by Pavel Rotmistrov, one-time Marshal of the Soviet Armoured Forces. He summed the situation up as follows:

'. . . only the tank, during the attack, has the ability to advance to within a short distance from the enemy and to destroy him at close range by its fire;

only the tank can carry out an uninterrupted attack, destroying in its advance (by fire and the use of its tracks) the points of resistance of the enemy which have survived the artillery preparation;

only the tank, which has cannon and machine-guns, has the ability in the attack to destroy most effectively all the anti-infantry means of battle, to fight against tanks and the artillery defence;

only the tank, thanks to its armour, can aggressively go into the attack without fear of machine-guns, automatic and rifle fire, and also the fire of light artillery, and has the ability to fight these defensive weapons on its own and by skilful action can emerge as the victor in this struggle;

only the tank, by having an engine and caterpillar tracks, can attack at great speed and destroy the enemy, before the latter can get ready to fight the tank . . .'

Another great Russian Tank Marshal, Malinovsky, wrote:

'. . . neither now, nor obviously in the future, are we able to

dispense with the tank. The tank has many remarkable combat features which allow the successful execution of combat tasks in a nuclear war. Among all the other types of combat means, the tank alone is able to survive a nuclear burst, especially the shock wave and dangerous radiation. This is a very important attribute in modern conditions. In addition, the tank has high mobility, firepower and striking force. . . . Many tasks still have to be executed by conventional firepower. Tanks are the best means for this. Thus, the tank-type combat vehicle will remain in service with our Army. . . .'

The Arab-Israeli War of 1967 really convinced a great number of people that the armoured arm was still the dominant offensive weapon. I personally think that this war should be analysed in the same light as the Spanish Civil War, i.e. that it is not indicative of a future conflict between major armies in Europe. The terrain and visibility in the Six Day War were completely alien to those of Europe, and lent themselves greatly to the broad manoeuvres of mechanized units. This does not mean, however, that the armoured arm will not remain the dominant offensive weapon in such a war, since it is, under any circumstances, still the fastest and most cost-

During the inter-war period most countries experimented with six-wheeled armoured cars. The vehicle below, an American T-4, was typical of this kind of vehicle although it never entered production. Britain made extensive use of such cars.

effective means of achieving military aims. From experiences of previous wars, however, it is very likely that the form of a future conflict will be as novel as the *Blitzkrieg* was in World War II, but what form this will take is impossible to foresee. The only reason for mentioning this is that it is so easy to put one's faith in a weapon which achieved good results in a past conflict, and to take it for granted that it would be equally effective in the next. The effect that the tank had in World War I may well be achieved in World War III by some other weapon system. The secret of the effectiveness of such a weapon as the tank lies in its element of surprise; the enemy of World War I was unprepared for the tank; the enemy of World War II was unprepared for *Blitzkrieg* war. . . . But the enemy in World War III?

This form of approach is negative in its entirety, since it suggests no alternative, or even direction of search to find an alternative. So long as all armies develop the tank and other types of armoured fighting vehicles, then their value

At the beginning of the war the Russians possessed rather inferior armoured car models, but towards 1944 improved types appeared. The BA-64 (*below*) was one of the later types.

will be assured. We must also bear in mind that, for the first time in the history of warfare, it has been possible to combine the three basic factors – firepower, protection and manoeuvrability – into one weapon system. This is significant in that, with such a combination, only sophistication and not replacement will follow. So long as we define the tank as a materialistic representation of these three factors, then the tank will exist for as long as war itself exists. Whether the tank has wheels, tracks, or some other means of mobility, whether it has steel armour or some form of force-field, whether it has a conventional gun or some futuristic 'ray' gun – the combination will be there!

It is generally agreed that, whatever the conditions, the ultimate aim in war is to occupy the enemy's ground as fast and as effectively as possible. One can bomb indefinitely but, unless actually occupied by armed personnel, the vanquished, given time, will rise out of the ashes and strike back. The ultimate military aim in war, therefore, is to deploy infantry in the enemy area and the tank is the infantryman's closest supporting weapon, accompanying him everywhere he goes to reduce the opposition to a minimum. By placing the

The Germans made extensive use of armoured cars during the war, and the 4-wheel drive (and steering) Horch model (*below*) was typical. Faceted armour was common on German armoured cars.

infantryman and his other supporting arms – artillery, engineers, signals, etc. – in armoured fighting vehicles they are guaranteed a degree of immunity from all types of weapons, including nuclear weapons. When in the final assault the infantry have to leave the cover of their carrier vehicles, it is the role of the tank to ensure that they achieve the final phase – the occupation and control of enemy territory.

Today there is a whole range of armoured fighting vehicles, built for various purposes, and sometimes it becomes almost impossible to distinguish between them. When the tank first appeared it was easy: there was only the tank and the armoured car – one having tracks and the other having wheels. Now we have armoured scout cars, armoured cars, armoured personnel carriers, tanks, self-propelled artillery, missile carriers, load-carriers, amphibious tractors, engineer vehicles and many, many more. These may be wheeled, tracked, semi-tracked, wheel-cum-tracked, or some other configuration. Those which are wheeled may be 4-, 6-, 8- or even 10-wheeled; those that are tracked might have 2 or 4 separate track systems, or even 4 arranged with 2 in parallel on each side. With such permutations and combinations it is

The US White scout car (*below*) was the standard US armoured car at the beginning of the war. Although it did not play a significant part, it served as the basis for a series of half-tracked vehicles.

no wonder that people find themselves incapable of distinguishing between them. Since there is no standard method known to be available, I will put forward a simple rule which may be used to identify types of vehicles. To say that an armoured car is wheeled and that a tank is tracked is not in itself a truism; certain French and US armoured cars of the 'thirties were fully-tracked, and during the last war both the US and the Germans used half-tracked armoured cars. Any attempt, therefore, to classify types of vehicles according to visual or technological features is not possible. One must analyse each system according to its tactical role and the balance between its mobility, firepower and protection.

Firstly, every type of vehicle has a military role to perform. The main types are as follows:

The *armoured car* is a reconnaissance or liaison vehicle, and is offensive only as a last resort. Its prime mission is to gain information or to liaise between various units; for this reason it must be extremely mobile, difficult to detect, and capable of retreating (or going to ground) under fire. Hence most armoured cars are small, making them difficult to detect, have very light armour and armament, and an automotive train enabling them to move as fast as possible (hence most are wheeled).

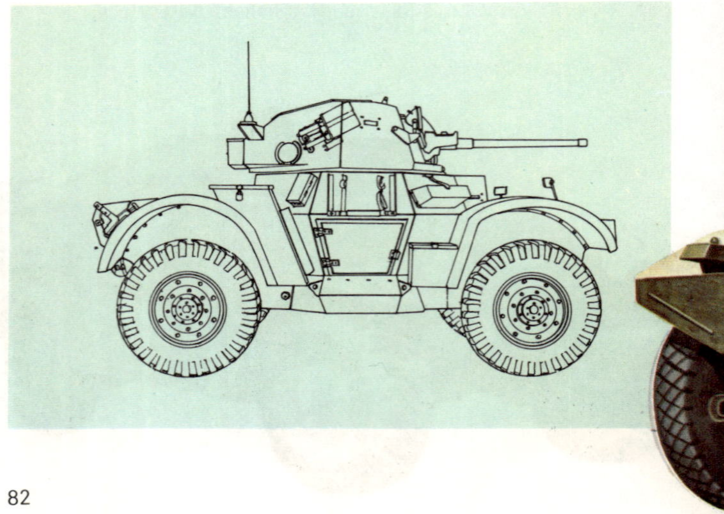

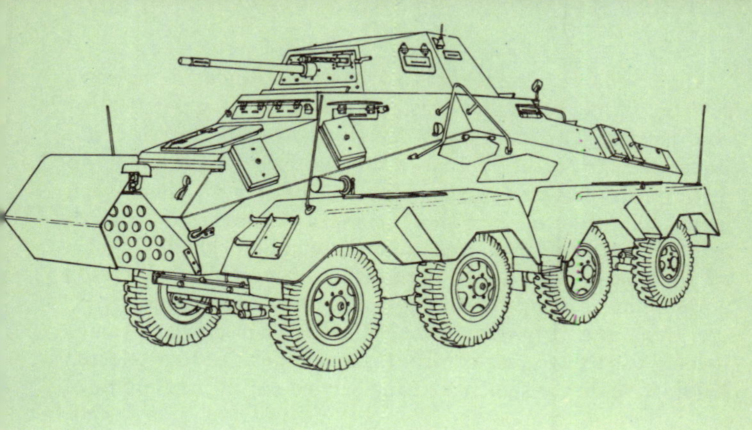

British armoured cars produced during the war were undoubtedly superior to any other models. They were squat, well-armoured and armed, and had good performance. The Daimler on the left was one of the most common. The German 8-wheeled armoured car, shown above, was an exceptional vehicle ideally suited to desert warfare. It was, however, very high, and expensive to produce. The Panhard AMD 35 armoured car (*below*) was a standard French armoured car at the start of the war.

The *armoured personnel carrier* (or *armoured infantry vehicle*) is one particular class which causes a great deal of controversy. The tactics and design of armoured carriers has fluctuated so greatly, that attempts have been made to distinguish between various models by giving them such names as armoured personnel carriers, mechanized infantry combat vehicles, armoured infantry combat vehicles, and a whole host of others. All these rather obscure and confusing designations attempt to distinguish between two basic types; the first, the original armoured personnel carrier, was a vehicle used purely to transport men under fire to a selected point. Here they disembarked and carried out the final phase of

For a long time the Americans dispensed with the armoured car, but recently they have adopted the Commando (*below*) which has good mobility and is amphibious. The fact that it can carry several armed men means it can be used as an armoured personnel carrier.

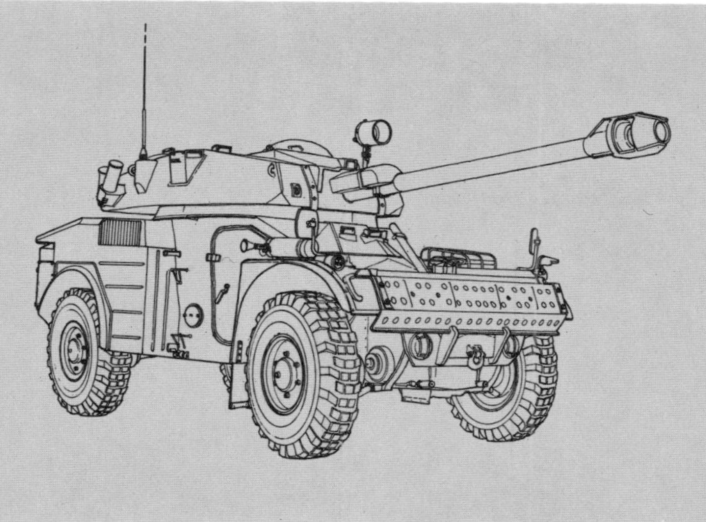

One of the leading contemporary armoured car designs is the French Panhard AML (*above*), which can be fitted out with a multiplicity of weapons, ranging from machine-guns to anti-tank missiles. The vehicle shown has a 90 mm. anti-tank gun.

the attack on foot. (Mr. R. M. Ogorkiewicz, the celebrated authority on armoured fighting vehicles, has aptly described these as 'battle taxis'.) A later concept – arising principally from American experience in Vietnam – was that of the 'mechanized infantry fighting vehicle'. Unlike the former type, this vehicle is intended to carry infantry right through an attack and therefore has inboard facilities for the use of weapons from the vehicle. This latter concept, however, is not very practical, since it destroys the prime advantage of the infantryman – his ability to disperse and occupy ground. Such vehicles are ultimately iterating toward a new concept of tank, one capable of operating in close country and capable of defending itself against localized attacks by infantry. It does seem as if the problem of the armoured infantry fighting vehicle will never be satisfactorily resolved.

The two armoured cars currently in service with the British Army. The Ferret (*below*) is a very light and small armoured car with a very good cross-country performance. Several versions exist, including a special variant which can fire anti-tank guided missiles. The perforated device fitted to the front is called a 'sand channel' and is used to help the vehicle out of slippery terrain. The Saladin (*bottom*) is a very powerful vehicle mounting a 76 mm. gun, and its six equally-spaced wheels give it a good cross-country performance. It is, however, extremely high. Both these vehicles are to be replaced by the new range of armoured vehicles, one of which is illustrated on page 69.

The *self-propelled weapon system* is more or less self-explanatory. It is a vehicle which provides mobility and *reasonable* protection from a particular weapon. Today, the immense number and range of weapons (anti-tank guns, anti-tank rockets, mortars, howitzers, field guns, flame-throwers, anti-aircraft missiles/guns, etc.) make the provision of this type of vehicle a nightmare. It is for this reason that attempts have been made to standardize one chassis which may be simply modified to mount any particular weapon. Such chassis are usually those used for the armoured infantry vehicle. Although the British carried out a great deal of experimentation with this type of vehicle, it was really the Germans, with their concept of the Panzer Division, who made it an indispensable category of armoured fighting vehicle.

The *tank* is a unique vehicle, in that it is capable of supporting infantry in the attack and of destroying enemy tanks and other armoured fighting vehicles, with the *maximum* chance of survival. Here, there is an equal balance between the firepower, mobility and protection requirements. In other words, whereas most other vehicles are biased tactically toward one or two of the fundamental characteristics, the tank on the other hand satisfies all three factors equally. In the design of a tank one cannot say that any particular factor is more important fundamentally than any other. We may therefore define a tank as a system which is designed to achieve the best possible balance between these three factors.

We discussed earlier, in the simple case of the boxer, how it is not physically possible to produce a system that has the best of everything, since firepower and protection are directly proportional to weight, and mobility is inversely proportional to weight. For this reason, in the design of a tank, a certain compromise must be made. One must define a minimum required speed and performance to determine the minimum allowable power-to-weight-ratio. The power-to-weight-ratio varies with the size and type of engine which is used. In the case of a tank, there is a limit to the width, defined by railway transportation requirements (variable with a particular country). With a tracked vehicle – as the tank to date has always been – there is a certain range of values for the L/C ratio (steering ratio), which is defined as:

The Laffly S-15 armoured personnel carrier illustrated above was one of the earliest wheeled APCs taken into service. It was used by the French Army up until the Second World War. It had an extremely good cross-country performance.

$$\frac{\text{Length of track on the ground}}{\text{Width between track centres.}}$$

If the L/C ratio is less than, or exceeds this range, then the tank will not steer. (Certain clever designs have been tried which overcome this problem – such as the linked vehicle and the curved-track steered vehicle, but what they gain in this respect is little compared with what has been lost in others.) The sheer physical size of a tank is, therefore, restricted. As a result there is a maximum limit to the size of engine which may be employed, and at the same time the associated cooling and fuel systems, etc. It has been found with conventional internal-combustion engines that the limit of engine power is 1,000 HP. Before even attempting to design a tank, therefore, we have imposed certain constraints. The output of this engine governs the power-to-weight-ratio,

The Russians made great use of amphibious vehicles, and the BAZ (*above*) was the only vehicle of this type to be adopted by any army. It was a conversion of the standard BA-32 armoured car, being propelled in water by a screw.

which in turn governs the weight. There is a choice of power-to-weight ratios, depending on what speed is considered to be necessary. This is practically the only degree of freedom in tank design and hence, is where most controversy arises. Some nations, particularly those who paid the price for limited mobility during the Second World War, have since been so biased the other way that they consider mobility to be the most important factor in tank design. If, however, one takes a rational approach to tank design, it is easy to see that this is not necessarily true.

In the first instance, mobility means cross-country movement, and it is here that high power-to-weight-ratios become of prime importance. The limiting factors in fast cross-country travel are not, however, so much the availability of power but to an equal extent the abilities to:

Because of the advantage on roads, many armies have built armoured personnel carriers on wheeled chassis. The Dutch DAF YP-408, produced during the late 'fifties, is a good example. It is currently in service with the Dutch Army.

a) provide a smooth ride (e.g. to have an effective suspension system);
b) be able to select required gear ranges almost instantaneously;
c) be able to steer under all conditions.

If any of these conditions are not satisfactorily fulfilled then, irrespective of the speed which a tank can actually achieve on level ground (or roads), the cross-country speed is limited. In the conventional tank the limiting cross-country speed is of the order of 20 mph on average, but there have been experimental models which can achieve much higher speeds. Such high speeds have been made available by the use of e.g. hydro-pneumatic suspension systems, automatic or infinitely variable gearboxes, and specially designed tracks. Such innovations, however, produce complications in other important fields, such as:

a) requiring extra volume inside the tank;
b) extra production costs;
c) reduced reliability;
d) increased vulnerability;
e) complex maintenance requirements.

Furthermore, the increases in performance with such innovations have not been of such an order as to significantly increase the speed. The fact that a tank moves at 30 mph rather than 20 mph under combat conditions is not so very important. It is not much more difficult to hit a tank moving at 30 mph than one moving at 20 mph (particularly since it will invariably be moving towards you!), and often tank speeds are limited by the overall rate of advance of a force – which ultimately is limited by the rate at which information is received and analysed, the speed at which orders can be received and executed, and the holding capability of a defender. Indeed, there are a great many more factors which govern the approach speed, but in any event it is clear that the benefits to be gained by such innovations compared with conventional systems are minimal and are only achieved at a high price in other respects. The only case for fast tank speeds is for strategic movement, that is movement from front to front. In the past this has been achieved by the use of special 'tank transporters' or railway wagons which can

Although the Russians have several models of tracked armoured personnel carriers, during the 'sixties they adopted this BTR-60P 8-wheeler. This vehicle is fully amphibious and several versions exist, including one model with a turret.

certainly transport tanks at speeds several times those of the fastest tank. On the other hand, driving tanks over long strategic distances incurs excessive wear and tear upon the automotive components and inevitably makes them incapable of operation without excessive maintenance.

There are, therefore, two main lines of thought in tank design:

a) that which stipulates a certain weight in order to achieve a high speed;
b) that which allows greater weight and achieves a speed compromise.

Tanks which are designed to satisfy (a) invariably appear with reduced armour protection, since this is the most economic means of decreasing weight. Tanks which are designed to satisfy (b) are able to don thicker armour, without at the same time – from a tactical view – losing the advantages which the former model possesses. The basic design of a tank, there-

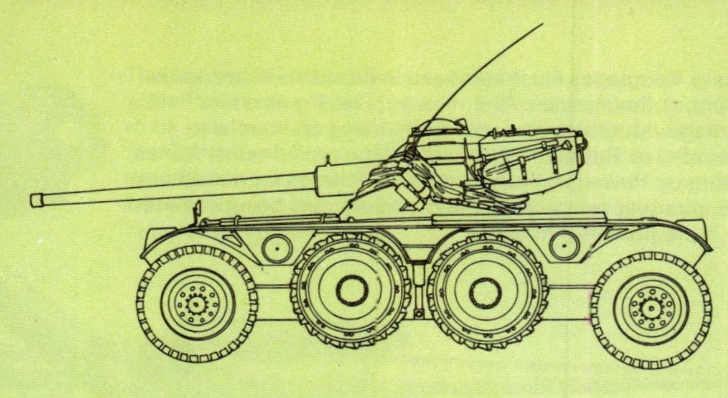

fore, has certain technological constraints, ranked in order of preference or priority:

TANK A	TANK B
Mobility	Firepower
Firepower	Armour Protection
Armour Protection	Mobility

The ultimate deciding factor is what task or role do we envisage our tank executing? Just because one country adopts a lightly-armoured fast tank, and the other a heavily-armoured slow tank, there is no legitimate reason why both cannot be right simultaneously. For example, let us look at the requirements of two of the leading tank-using nations, namely the Soviet Union and Great Britain:

Britain was the first country after the Second World War to adopt a wheeled armoured personnel carrier. The Saracen (*left*) was based on the same chassis as the Saladin armoured car illustrated on page 86. The Panhard 8-wheeled EBR armoured car (*above*) is a most interesting vehicle. Its original design was conceived as early as 1940 when one experimental vehicle was actually built. The four wheels grouped in the centre are hydraulically raised for road travel and may be lowered for cross-country use. The model above uses the same turret as the AMX-13 light tank (illustrated on page 62). An armoured personnel carrier version also exists.

SOVIET UNION	GREAT BRITAIN
Doctrine of offence;	Doctrine of defence;
Requires large strategic movement;	Requires relatively small strategic movement;
Requires large concentrations of tanks;*	Size of tank force restricted by budgetary allowance and manpower limitations;
Requires high level of automotive efficiency;	Requires relatively low level of automotive efficiency.

* According to Lanchester, an attacker must have a force size at least three times that of the defender (everything else equal) in order to achieve parity. Even a 50:50 chance is not sufficient, and so the Russians require relatively large numbers of tanks.

From these constraints it may be seen, therefore, that the Soviet Union requires tanks that have a good offensive capability (e.g. effective weapons). Their tanks must also be

The half-track is a vehicle which received great attention. The Martel light tank (*below*) was by no means the first but is nevertheless a very interesting vehicle. Developed in the 'thirties it was intended as a cheap tank to be built in quantity.

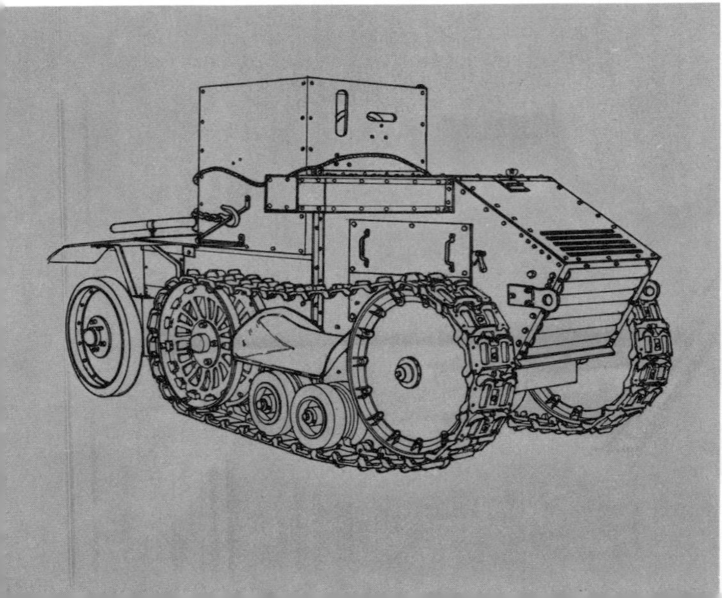

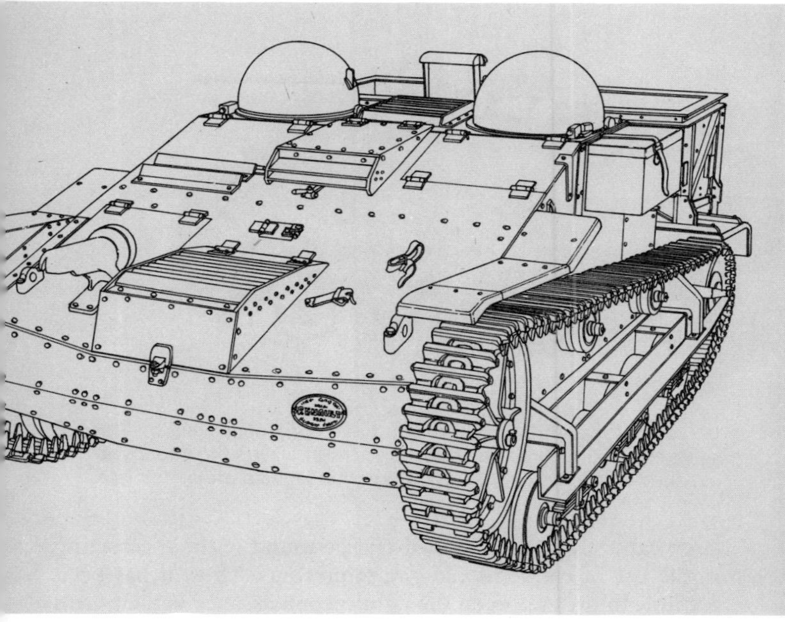

The French adopted the design of the Carden-Loyd carrier shortly after its appearance, and the Renault U.E. (*above*) was employed by their army for a multiplicity of tasks. The armoured domes, used to protect the crew, could be folded back.

which could be employed was restricted by the maximum possible turret-ring diameter. This in turn was governed by the width of the tank, which itself was dependent (as mentioned earlier) upon railway gauges. Since the Germans utilized a railway gauge which was several inches greater than that of the British, they were always capable of mounting more powerful guns. This rather obscure fact was the underlying reason for continual development and replacement of tank models on the part of the British during the Second World War.

The introduction of the ATGW (anti-tank guided weapon), on the other hand, has provided a means of delivering a

(*Above*) a modern US Mechanized Infantry Fighting Vehicle. This is similar to an armoured personnel carrier but allows the infantry to use their weapons from the vehicle with adequate protection from enemy fire.

large-calibre HESH or shaped-charge round without resorting to the use of conventional gun mountings. Thus, it has been possible to provide even the light reconnaissance vehicle with a significant anti-tank capability, without fundamental alterations to its basic design.

The existence of the Soviet IS–III/T–10 heavy tank family forced the British to produce a vehicle capable of defeating it at normal ranges of engagement. Initially, a design study was carried out to mount a 183 mm. HESH-firing gun on both a Conqueror and a Centurion chassis. During final stages of experimentation with prototypes, which did not prove to be tactically successful due to their limited mobility and other encumberances, the introduction of the guided weapon provided an alternative solution. The first vehicle specifically designed to fire such a weapon was the FV–4010, based on the Centurion tank. This vehicle was lighter than the Centurion and, for reasons which will be explained later, provided superior destructive potential to the 183 mm. proposal.

The only remaining advantage of the heavy gun tank over the light guided-weapon launcher vehicle was its better immunity to conventional attack; however, the lethality of

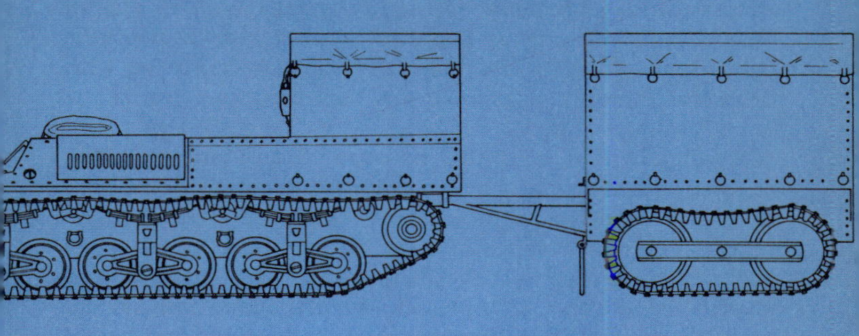

Before the war, the French employed special vehicles to carry equipment and ammunition. The vehicle illustrated above was the Lorraine 38L, shown towing a tracked armoured trailer.

the HESH and shaped-charge weapons made it difficult, if not impossible, to achieve this. In conjunction with the restricted mobility, difficulties of transportation and high cost, therefore, the heavy tank is no longer an economic surety.

This leaves us with the medium tank. Overall, the standardization of one tank class not only reduces cost and resupply problems, but also means that production can be concentrated on the one tank model as against two, or even three. In Britain, following the war, it was proposed to build the medium, or 'battle' tank, as the 'Universal Tank', a maid of all work. This was, apart from its original role as an infantry-support and anti-tank means, to execute the other vital functions of tanks, such as engineer vehicles, mine-clearing tanks, etc. Development in Britain proceeded along these lines and terminated in the FV–200 series – which tended to the heavy, rather than the medium, class tank. The Centurion, however, was considered to be the superior model in overall mobility, and new methods of mounting weapons showed that it was capable of considerable up-gunning. The FV–200, developed into the Conqueror heavy tank, has since been phased out, and the current Chieftain is intended to carry out the roles of both the Centurion and the Conqueror, having almost equivalent armour to the heavy tank with an overall weight (and that means mobility) approaching that of the Centurion. Weighing less than fifty tons (as compared with sixty-five for the Conqueror), this tank mounts a gun of the same calibre (120 mm.).

Development in the United States and Russia followed along different lines. Briefly, the Russians had managed to produce both a medium and a heavy tank family as early as 1940, several years in advance of other nations, namely the T–34 and the KV. It seems that they came to a rather interesting and positive conclusion. By freezing advanced development and research they could achieve two things; firstly, they could produce very large quantities of both of these models, and secondly all the automotive deficiencies (e.g. in transmission, engine, suspension, etc.) could be rectified, thereby providing a fairly reliable tank family. This they have certainly done; by mass-producing modified versions of these two tanks they

After the war, most nations began to adopt tracked armoured personnel carriers. The first to place a vehicle in production were the Americans, followed closely by the British. (*Below*) US M-113; (*below right*) British FV-432.

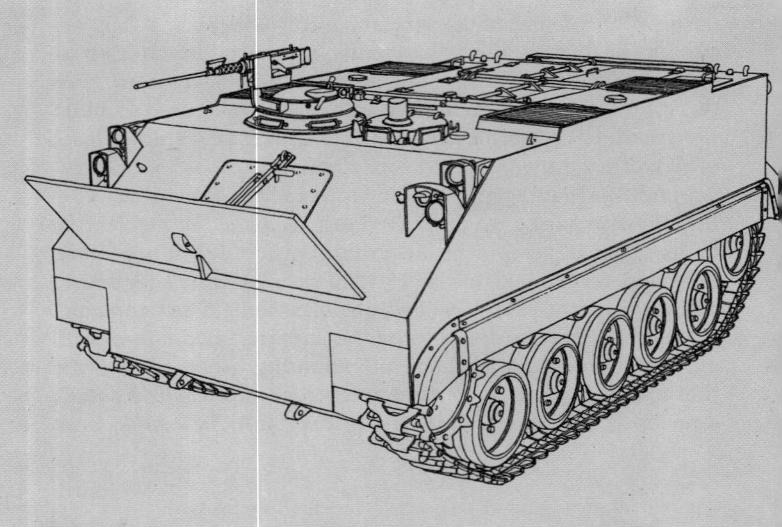

have assured that any technological inferiorities in their models, as compared with other nations, will be counter-balanced by numerical superiority. At the same time, a high degree of reliability and standardization of components ensures that a maximum quantity of tanks are battleworthy at any moment in time, even after very long strategic marches. They also, of course, have few problems with spares and re-supply. Let us not think, however, that these unsophisticated models are not capable of satisfactorily engaging and destroying our 'armoured computers'. Even though they have kept scientific development to a minimum, they have not neglected improvements to the weapons systems and associated equipment. Further, *all* their tanks have a built-in amphibious or deep wading capability, with a small delay time in preparation, although this is still restricted to a greater degree by the difficulties of egress on unprepared river crossings. They also had service-fitted infra-red night-driving and fighting equipment when other countries were still experimenting with the idea!

The United States, on the other hand, have made such considerable advances in weapons and armour technology that they may well balance out this numerical superiority. Briefly, these developments are as follows:

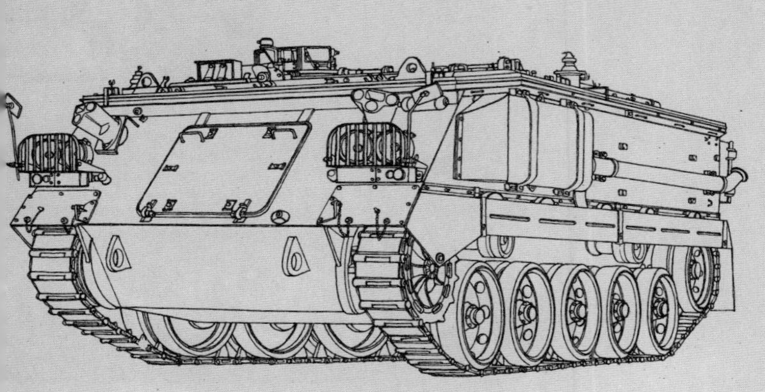

a) the third generation anti-tank missile system;
b) light-weight armour which might eventually provide immunity to both kinetic-energy and shaped-charge attack;
c) hydro-pneumatic suspension systems, which improve performance across country and allow reductions in tank heights.

As regards the other nations now producing armoured fighting vehicles, they do not seem to have the right attitude

towards tank design, or indeed an understanding of the requirements for a tank. At present both the French and the Germans have gone to the extreme of lightly armouring their tanks in order to increase mobility – a fact arising from their experiences during the Second World War, where, at one stage or another, both nations paid dearly in mobility for excess in armour protection. The use of certain complicated low-velocity hollow-charge rounds involves difficulties in kill accuracy, which will be discussed later. The new prototypes of the joint German/US main battle tank are theoretically very good, but, by virtue of their complexity, suffer from high failure rates and are extremely expensive to produce. The German Leopard tank is quite good in comparison with other models, and compares favourably with the Soviet T–54 but, in the numerical quantity now available, lacks the killing power necessary to defeat substantial numbers of enemy tanks.

The Swedish S–Tank has aroused considerable interest with its rather novel design layout. It is interesting that, as early as 1953–4, the British experimented with a very similar vehicle utilizing a hydro-pneumatic suspension system as a means of traversing and elevating the gun. The reasons for not continuing development, however, were that the ability to track a target and lay-on the main armament were not as good as the

The Canadian Lynx (*above left*) was a close copy of the British Daimler scout car. It is a good example of a well-designed, 4-wheel-drive, armoured reconnaissance car. (*Left*) the new Soviet armoured infantry vehicle, which at the time of its appearance was a most revolutionary vehicle. It is amphibious, has a 76 mm. gun and a machine-gun and can fire anti-tank guided missiles. The crew can fire their weapons from inside the vehicle.

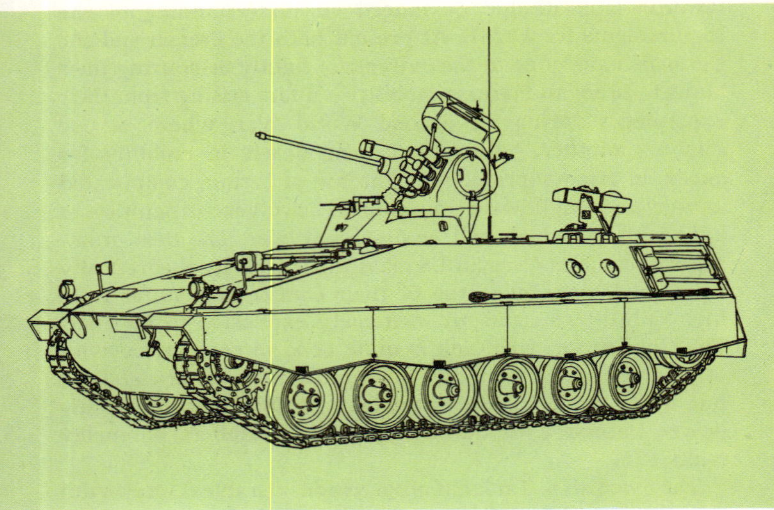

conventional mounting (in fact, on the move it is impossible). Furthermore, reliance upon the running gear, engine, suspension, and just about every other component in the tank for engagement with the main weapon is most unwise. It implies that the tank cannot engage if there are any malfunctions in any of these systems, which would prove a considerable disadvantage. The conventional tank can still engage targets totally unimpaired by such defects. There are, of course, considerable advantages in utilizing this layout – firstly, the hydro-pneumatic suspension enables the overall height of the vehicle to be reduced (which means it is less likely to be detected and very difficult to hit), and it also enables the tank to be controlled from all positions; secondly, the rigid mounting of the armament in the glacis plate not only reduces the overall height by the absence of a turret, but also means that a powerful gun can be mounted in a relatively small vehicle. This layout also simplifies the problems of automatic loading, even if round selection is required.

ARMAMENT

One role of the tank is the support of infantry, and it must therefore have a weapon (or weapons) capable of giving this to a maximum. The two available means to date, as far as is known, are the machine-gun and a high-explosive firing gun. Again, the tank has the important role of destroying tanks and must have a weapon capable of all known forms of armour at normal combat ranges (between 500 and 2,000 yards), at the same time ensuring a high first round hit probability.

(*Left*) the new German Marder (Spider) armoured infantry vehicle is of exceptionally good design. The 20 mm. cannon on top of the turret can be fired by remote-control, as can the smaller machine-gun at the rear of the vehicle. (*Below*) a rather unique armoured infantry vehicle is the Swedish Pbv.302. This is fully amphibious and has a number of advanced features. It utilizes components of the S-tank (see pages 64–65). The turret on the off-side mounts a heavy machine-gun.

Firstly, the attachment of machine-guns to tanks presents no problems which have not been satisfactorily overcome. Again, the performance of high-explosive rounds such as HESH and canister are reasonable in the role of destroying personnel and static targets.

It may be appreciated, that in the case of a 'hard' target (i.e. an armoured one) which is moving, say, at 20 mph, it is very difficult to deduce the range and speed of the target. To reduce the required corrections for azimuth and elevation when engaging a moving target, it is necessary to have either of two types of rounds:

a) a high-velocity round with a very small flight time, thereby reducing errors in azimuth and elevation;

b) a slow round which can be controlled in flight in order to guide it towards the target until contact occurs.

In the first case, the only available round able to perform this satisfactorily is the Sabot – or armour-piercing, kinetic-energy round. The extremely high velocity of this round enables high probabilities of hit in both azimuth and elevation. On average, at normal ranges of engagement, a Sabot aimed at the glacis plate of a sideways moving tank (i.e. the worst case) will reach the target before the latter has travelled its own length, thereby ensuring a hit. Further, the drop in elevation of the shot is so small that it is possible to bracket target ranges into three basic categories – called 'dots'. This requires the gunner to assess the range accurate to the nearest

The difficulties associated with the Allied landings necessitated the use of a number of specialized tanks. The Canal Defence Light (*left*) consisted of a powerful searchlight mounted in the turret of a General Grant tank. The gun was a dummy to confuse the enemy. (*Right*) the Valentine bridge-layer, which was used to aid tanks in crossing wide trenches.

500 yards, and does not require the use of complicated and time-consuming devices such as optical range-finders and ballistic computers. To ensure that this bracketing is assessed even more accurately, the three-stage ranging machine-gun aids the commander or gunner to make his decision in a relatively small interval of time. No doubt, the perfection of the laser range-finder will revolutionize tank gunnery, since it is a very quick and accurate aid in assessing both the range and speed of the target vehicle.

The necessity for first-round kills and minimum engagement time may be appreciated when one considers the numerical superiority of the assumed enemy, whereby it becomes necessary to destroy about fifteen tanks to even up the odds. In addition it is necessary to stop the tank to fire, and it is the normal tactical manoeuvre to halt, fire, and then move off as soon as possible. If the tank deploys to fire several rounds it is a stationary target and virtually a sitting duck! In the same manner, the longer it takes to leash-off an aimed round, the longer the tank is stationary and the higher the probability of being hit by another tank. Thus, the faster the gunner can select, assess, and engage the target (at the same time ensuring a high kill probability) the more tanks that can be successfully destroyed, and the higher is

One of the major threats to the tank during World War II was the land-mine. A common expedient for clearing lanes through minefields for tanks was the mine-roller, featured above as an attachment to the Matilda tank, and the flail (*below right*) fitted to the Sherman tank. The roller device simulated the weight of a tank in an attempt to detonate mines, whilst the flail, driven from the tank engine, beat the ground like a series of hammers. Even so, it was a dangerous and time-consuming operation, and tricks could be used to counter such devices. The carpet device, shown below fitted to the Churchill tank, was laid over soft ground to assist the passage of vehicles, particularly of the wheeled type.

the survival probability of that tank during combat.

In the second case, the guided weapon ensures a high kill probability by utilizing the superior penetrating qualities of the shaped-charge or HESH warhead, together with control of the system in flight. There are, however, several disadvantages with this system; it is essentially a line-of-sight weapon and has a minimum controllable range. Also the time of flight will probably never reduce to the level of that of the Sabot round, which means a relatively longer engagement time. This time is dependent upon the ability to see the missile in flight. The velocity of the missile must be sufficiently low in order that the operator can track it during flight, as well as to enable it to be stabilized in the direction of the target. (With the second generation missile system, where all that is necessary is for the gunner to track the target through his graticule, and the third-generation system, still under development, where the missile seeks out its own target, much higher velocities will be possible. Even the second-

generation system, however, has proved to be extremely temperamental and unreliable and exists only as a future possibility.) With the present system, therefore, the time of flight may be as long as 30–40 seconds (as against 1·5 seconds for a Sabot over the same range), after which time the target may no longer be visible, and the gunner is unable to acquire and engage a second target for a significantly long period of time. A technical problem with guided-missiles is that they are complete rounds, and they restrict loading time through their bulk and weight. This also decreases the quantity which can be stowed inside a tank to a very low value. The separate loading (i.e. propellent and shot are separate from each other) APDS and HESH rounds, especially when assisted by a ramming device, ensure a high rate of fire and also adequate

Because of the cost and rarity of tanks, it became necessary to salvage knocked-out or broken-down vehicles under fire. The Allies made great use of armoured recovery vehicles, which were conventional tanks modified for the retrieval of immobilized vehicles. The Churchill ARV portrayed above was a standard British version with a dummy turret and gun. An A-frame was mounted at the rear of the vehicle over which passed a hawser driven from a special engine in the static turret.

stowage within the tank. Furthermore, immersion of conventional rounds in inert media reduces fire risk, a facility which could not be accomplished easily in the case of guided weapons.

Of course, as has been mentioned earlier, the guided-weapon launcher has distinct weight advantages over the conventional gun, but it is worth outlining the developments in gun mountings which are gradually enabling more powerful guns to be mounted in lighter vehicles.

The first simple means of up-gunning a tank is the limited-traverse or case-mate mounting. This is where the gun is mounted in the hull. The hull and suspension are much more capable of absorbing the tremendous recoil loadings of powerful guns than a turret where all the energy is transmitted to

The Americans and the British also modified the Sherman tank for use as an armoured recovery vehicle, which was of similar design to the Churchill type. Special tools and equipment were carried to enable rapid maintenance and retrieval of disabled vehicles. Although the Germans and the Japanese made a number of ARV versions they did not use them to the same extent as the Allies. The most common German model was that based on the Panther tank. The Germans used a special half-track version.

the turret ring. In the case of earlier turreted tanks, the size of the turret ring governed the power of the gun which could be mounted. A too-powerful gun would split the turret ring in half. With the limited traverse mounting this problem is overcome, but the inability to freely traverse the gun is a great disadvantage. The tank has here lost a complete degree of freedom and becomes vulnerable under certain tactical situations.

The next crucial development was made by the French. The French experimented with 'oscillating' turrets, which provided a means of transmitting recoil loadings to the hull through special trunnions. The gun was rigidly mounted in the turret and had no mantlet. Apart from requiring a 20% increase in turret weight, this design was extremely vulnerable. Even well-placed small-arms fire could blister the turret to the extent of rendering it immobile. With the advances made in technology, rigid gun mounting in conventional turrets, together with advances in reducing barrel

Although not strictly tanks, a number of radio-controlled armoured vehicles have been used from time to time. Shown below is the Japanese Nagayama tank tried out in the 'thirties.

weight, recoil loadings, etc., it has been possible to mount more powerful weapons in normal turrets with considerable success.

In the conventional tank the turret ring becomes the 'Achilles Heel', and it is vital that it should be protected to the maximum. In the past, due to the limited size of turret rings, greater turret space was obtained by the use of hexagonal designs (the first model so-designed being the British Covenanter tank). These turrets had undercut sides which tended to deflect shots to the turret ring. Such undercuts are aptly termed 'shell traps'. For some reason, these undercut turrets continue to be made; the Americans utilize the design in their Sheridan light tank, and the British in the Scorpion and Fox reconnaissance vehicles.

Whilst on the subject of turrets and armament, there are a few points of interest which appear to cause general confusion. In the first place, the introduction of the stabilizer for the main armament was *not*, as commonly thought, to enable tanks

During World War II, the Germans used operationally a number of remote-controlled and radio-controlled miniature tanks. These were usually filled with high-explosive and directed against enemy tanks or fortifications. The vehicle shown below is typical, and was called the 'Goliath'.

to engage on the move. They are not efficient enough to achieve this (bearing in mind that a first-round hit is required). Tanks lacking in this refinement have to have the gun locked to the rear of the hull when travelling fast or cross country, which means that considerable time is lost when halting in unfastening the gun, laying and firing. With the stabilizer, one is able to track a target whilst on the move to such an extent that the fine lay may be made on halting. It may, however, in the near future be possible to provide a tank with a stabilizer sensitive enough to allow it to fire whilst moving.

Secondly, even though fairly efficient automatic loading devices have been designed, there are two reasons why this has not been universally adopted. As stated earlier, the tank has a dual role; tank destruction and infantry support. Thus, at the minimum, two types of round are required, in fact

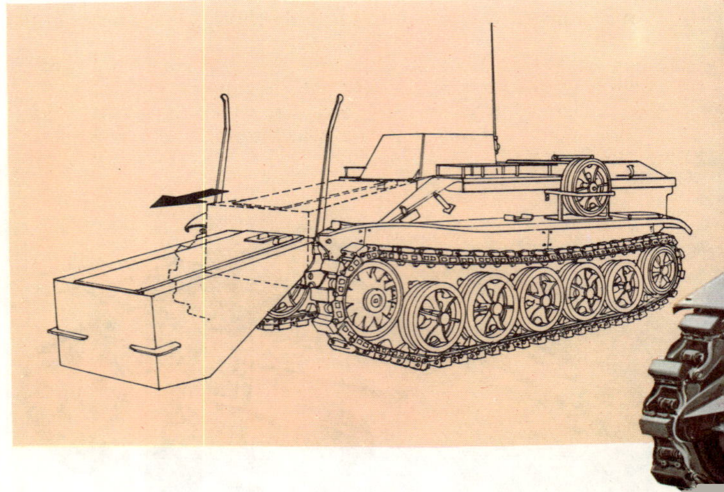

Towards the end of the war, the Germans were producing some very sophisticated versions of remote-controlled tanks and similar vehicles. The B-IV (*above*) was capable of being radio-controlled, but could also be driven by a man. A wedge-shaped block of explosive could be placed against an obstacle and the vehicle withdrawn to a safe distance before detonation.

anything up to five different types of round might be used. Since a magazine holds rounds loaded prior to engagement, the gunner has to use the round fed to the gun, and cannot select the one most suitable for that specific engagement. To cater for round selection it would be necessary to feed the gun from numerous independent magazines. As may be appreciated, not only does this present problems in engineering, but it also requires a great deal of vital space and necessitates the use of fixed rounds. Fixed rounds of the calibre currently in use are extremely awkward to handle and difficult to stow inside the tank. The most efficient loading system in use with large calibre rounds is a manual one with an automatic ram assist.

A similar vehicle to the B-IV was the NSU Springer (*below*) which was introduced very late in the war. This type of vehicle was peculiar to the Germans, although both the British and the Russians had developed similar vehicles. The Russians often removed the turrets from obsolescent light tanks and filled the hulls with explosives.

ARMOUR

The study of armour, unfortunately, is extremely technical and so specialized that it is difficult to obtain up-to-date literature on the subject. Basically, the armouring of a tank involves the following features:

a) the material to be used as armour, varying with the form of attack;
b) the method of fabricating the armoured hull and turret;
c) the weight limitation when deciding what part of the tank requires thicker armour than another;
d) the angle to which armour should be placed so as to afford maximum protection.

Materials utilized for armour are, at the moment, of two types:

a) those which provide protection from artillery high-explosive and small or large-calibre kinetic energy armour-piercing rounds;

The British and the Americans produced various light tank models for use in airborne operations. These were loaded into transport aircraft and gliders and took part in a number of operations. (*Left*) the American M-22 Locust light tank disembarking from a glider; (*above*) the British version, the Tetrarch light tank. An interesting feature of this vehicle is the novel method of steering; instead of varying the relative speeds of the tracks, the wheels were cleverly tilted to form the arc of an ellipse at the bottom and a straight line at the top. This was not altogether successful.

Due to the need for vehicles to take part in amphibious operations, special devices were used to enable tanks to float. Above is shown the Straussler screen which, together with a special propeller drive, enabled the tank to 'swim'.

b) those which provide protection from chemical energy armour-defeating projectiles.

The materials presently suitable for armour are the alloys of steel, titanium, aluminium and magnesium. Development with steel armour has progressed to the point where it is felt that future improvements will only be marginal. Titanium is very good, but it is both difficult to obtain and expensive. Aluminium armour came into use only after the Second World War and has certain advantages over other materials. High strength and high toughness are the major requirements for satisfactory armour, the former to resist penetration by

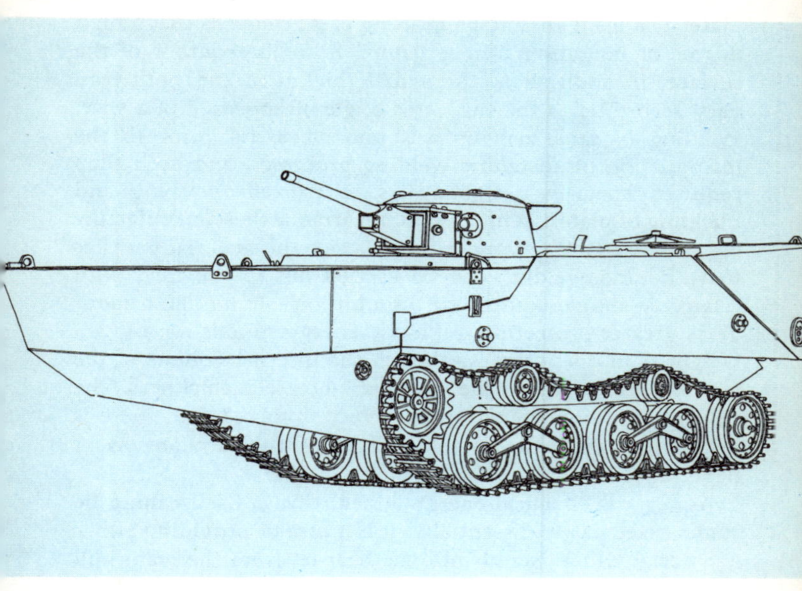

The Japanese operations were often conducted from, or against, Pacific islands or atolls. For this reason many of their tanks had amphibious capabilities. The version above had special wooden floats which could be blown off upon reaching dry land.

projectiles and the latter to prevent cracking-up and break-up of armour under impact. Density of the armour is important since it determines the weight available for a given application.

Due to the necessity for providing a bond as strong as the armour itself, original application to tanks was through rivetting. This bonding required highly accurate machining of plates, and when the armour was hit by projectiles rivets used to shear and fly about inside the tank. Casting of armour is a fairly successful process, but is extremely expensive and the results are not always predictable. Cast armour has been used in the manufacture of the Chieftain turret and glacis plate. The main advantage in using cast armour is that a high degree of immunity can be gained from the contour of the surface, in addition to the actual thickness, and both may vary according to the suspected angle of approach of a shot. Welding of tank armour was not successful prior to the introduction of austenitic welding processes, and even then required specially-designed jigs to prevent warping and buckling of plates. With aluminium armour these manufacturing problems are greatly reduced, since the material is easier to work and welding can be carried out in the field with relatively simple equipment. In addition, aluminium armour gives greater protection to kinetic-energy rounds for a given weight than does steel – although the internal volume of the tank is reduced due to the required increase in thickness. The subject of armour penetration is very involved, and there is insufficient space to go into details of the mechanisms of penetration.

As regards chemical-energy attack, this in itself cannot be summarized easily. Essentially, it is a case of providing either a material which 'stands-off' the heat jet from the main hull (i.e. spaced armour), or one which is not readily penetrated by heat jets to the extent of metallic armours. Silica and ceramic armours have reasonable heat-defeating qualities. Unfortunately, there seems to be no material which will resist both kinetic-energy and chemical-energy attacks.

In the case of kinetic-energy rounds, the inclination of the plate to the direction of impact greatly reduces penetration. The mechanism of penetration requires the shot to change direction; in doing this, it retains only a component of its original velocity and so effectiveness is reduced.

The Soviet Union has always devoted great attention to amphibious tanks. The multiplicity of lakes and marshes in the USSR make this type of vehicle an indispensable necessity. During the 'thirties much use was made of the T-37 light amphibious tank (*above*) which was based on a similar design by the British Vickers firm. The tank had special balsa-wood floats over the tracks and a propeller at the rear. It was particularly useful during the war with Finland. The most modern Soviet amphibious tank is the PT-76 (*below*) which is propelled in water by hydra-jets. The turret mounts a powerful 76 mm. gun. The chassis of this tank has been utilized for a whole range of specialized vehicles.

Without very complicated and bulky innovations, it is very difficult to make tanks float. Even with such devices it often occurs that tanks are 'blind' and unable to use their armament. With heavier tank models, therefore, one expedient was to make them travel beneath the water or wade. The British, and Russians, carried out experiments with 'snorkelling' tanks before the war. Both the Russians and the Germans used 'snorkelling' tanks operationally during the war. Above is shown the Churchill tank equipped with special pipes to allow it to wade up to the top of the hull. The vehicles were used during the unsuccessful Dieppe raid. Modern tanks, like the AMX-30 (*left*) have long snorkel tubes which allow the vehicles to drive along the bottom of a river. Some vehicles require special water-proofing before this is practicable, but all Russian service tanks are factory sealed and can go into action at a few minutes notice. Often the vehicles are guided to their destinations by an observer on the bank who gives directions over a radio. These tanks, however, have great difficulty in egressing and usually have to be towed out.

MOBILITY

Essentially, the mobility of a tank is dependent upon its automotive components. Starting from the ground upwards, it may be appreciated that mobility on hard flat road surfaces and mobility on rough, soft terrain are in no way interconnected. On roads, the smoothness and firmness of the surface enables a vehicle to move fast, it requiring little damping-out of vibration, and the mechanics of the terrain do not hinder significantly the conversion of tractive effort

Since tanks are primarily compromises between firepower, mobility and armour protection, it has often been necessary to produce special vehicles with increased firepower. The vehicle above was a special adaptation carried out by the French of their SOMUA medium tank. A high-velocity 75 mm. gun was mounted next to the driver, although the original armament in the turret was retained. Such tanks were intended to provide artillery fire support to armoured units. Not many such tanks were produced, although a similar vehicle was based on the Char B.

When the Germans occupied foreign territories in the war, they utilized practically every vehicle they could find in reasonable condition. A great number of these were converted into self-propelled weapons. One such conversion was the French Char B to mount a 105 mm. gun, illustrated below.

from the engine to the ground. Thus, the normal wheeled vehicle is adequate for road travel and at the moment can attain much higher speeds on roads than tracked vehicles. On soft, uneven terrain, however, the problems are entirely different; here the weight must be evenly distributed over the terrain so as to avoid sinkage, and the suspension must cater for rapid and exaggerated variations in terrain contour. In this case, the track is obviously superior. By providing a long flat area on the ground, the weight is evenly distributed over a large area and thus sinkage is less than in the case of the wheeled vehicle. Again, suspension systems utilizing several wheels can be made more sensitive to vibration and adequately damp-out the pitching, yawing and rolling motions of the vehicle. Thus a decision has to be made as to whether a particular type of vehicle is wheeled or tracked. The tank would be greatly limited to road networks if wheeled, and so it becomes imperative that it has tracks. Also, the great weight of armour and other components cannot be carried on a wheeled chasis as successfully as on a tracked one. Other disadvantages of wheeled vehicles have been mentioned earlier.

Various attempts have been made to achieve a balance between these two systems. In the case of pure-wheeled vehicles, the performance across country and the ability to ascend obstacles are proportional to the number of wheels

The use of rockets in war is no recent trend; even so, there have been some novel applications to armoured vehicles. The Russians in particular have utilized an extensive range of mobile rocket launchers, as have the Germans. A standardized German piece of equipment was that depicted above attached to the Sd.Kfz.251 armoured half-track. The rockets were launched from wooden cradles, in which they were transported.

used – so an eight-wheeled vehicle has a superior performance to a four-wheeled vehicle. In soft terrain, the problems of steering and conforming to changes in contour may be overcome by a linked vehicle. The linked vehicle steers by each component acting on the other to form a slewing or skidding action. Another solution is to combine wheels and tracks. The first such attempt was the half-track; this machine was fairly successful but does not compare with either wheeled or tracked systems on the respective terrains. Later, a vehicle known as the wheel-cum-track was evaluated; this vehicle usually has a system of hydraulic cylinders which enable the wheels to be raised or lowered. Thus the vehicle has the performance of an armoured car on roads, and that of a tank across country. This system is, however, extremely intricate and vulnerable, and has very great weight limitations. The hovercraft has fairly good cross-country ability, but is

One unsuccessful self-propelled weapon was the Russian KV-2, which was classified as an 'artillery tank' rather than a self-propelled gun. A powerful 152 mm. howitzer was mounted in an extremely high, unwieldy turret on a KV-1 tank chassis. The cumbersome turret presented great difficulties and sometimes, particularly on slopes, would not traverse. It was not long, therefore, before the Russians dispensed with the vehicle and introduced a limited traverse version.

restricted greatly in weight-carrying capability, and therefore cannot be easily armoured, and is not easily controlled in its present form.

As regards the fully-tracked vehicle, one of the major design problems is the provision of a reliable steering system. Practically all tracked vehicles produced so far steer either by slowing down one track and speeding the other up, or by braking one track. Various improvements upon these systems have been tried and many adopted in production vehicles. Perhaps the most common and most efficient is the controlled differential type, where power to the braked track is tapped-off to assist the moving one.

Next to the design and production of armour plate, and the science of armour penetration, tank steering represents one of the most complex factors in tank design.

The first really successful limited traverse self-propelled gun was the German *Sturmgeschütz* (*above*). Rather than being a clumsy improvisation, it was designed from the start as a mobile armoured infantry-support howitzer. The vehicle utilized the chassis and components of the German Pz.Kpfw.III medium tank and proved of immeasurable value in almost all campaigns fought by the German Panzer divisions. Later on it received a more powerful gun which could engage tanks.

The steering of a tank is also related to the type of gearbox employed. The problem with gearboxes generally is that they are usually 'step-down' systems, or ones which provide only a select range of speeds. During its motion across country a tank needs to change gear a very great number of times and so it is not surprising that various attempts have been made to provide more sophisticated gearboxes. The first significant improvement upon the conventional gearbox was the automatic type, which had the facility to change gear according to the characteristics of the terrain. The Americans made great use of the 'Hydramatic' transmission which behaved in this way. The main disadvantage of such a system was that it was not responsive to rapid terrain undulations, and by the time a particular ratio had been selected another was required. More sophisticated means of overcoming this problem were

When the pace of tank development during the war became so rapid that there existed a continual imbalance between armour and firepower, most countries adopted various compromises. One such improvization was to up-gun a tank by removing the turret and mounting the more powerful weapon in the hull. The Germans became masters of this technique and developed a series of tank-hunters called *Panzerjäger*. The model shown above was based on the Pz.IV and mounted a 75 mm. gun.

When the celebrated Tiger tank was in its design stage, two independent German automotive companies competed for contracts. One of these, headed by Dr Ferdinand Porsche, lost out but the chassis was utilized for a self-propelled 88 mm. anti-tank gun called 'Ferdinand', after its designer.

the application of hydraulic transmissions, which were first tried out as early as 1915, and the adoption of hydro-pneumatic suspensions. The hydraulic transmission utilizes oil pressure to drive the tracks, and since this is in itself infinitely variable, so are the ranges which could be obtained. Its main disadvantage was its extremely high sensitivity to driver reactions and the bulk required inside the tank. Hydro-pneumatic suspensions are still in the course of development and may eventually prove to be the answer. One means of overcoming the gear-changing problem is through the application of terrain sensors; these protrude from the front

One of the most famous Allied self-propelled guns was the M-7 (called 'Priest' by virtue of its pulpit-like direction tower). This vehicle, based on the famous Sherman tank, provided mobility for the 105 mm. howitzer, and saw action in the Western Desert and Europe.

of the vehicle and feed back to the suspension or gearbox the characteristics of the terrain ahead. Using this information, the particular system can adapt itself accordingly to correspond with the occurrence of the feature.

One method of overcoming the steering problem was through the application of the linked-hull principle. During the early 'twenties and 'thirties, an Italian engineer named Pavesi experimented with this type of vehicle. Essentially, it consists of two halves, each possessing an equal number of wheels, which are united through a central universal yoke. The linked vehicle is able to steer by acting on itself, so to speak. The front of the vehicle uses the rear part as a fulcrum when turning, and its steering characteristics are not quite as dependent on the terrain as is the case with the rigid tracked vehicle. It has been shown that the best conventional means of steering either a tracked or wheeled vehicle in soft muddy

To provide the Panther tank with a deadly anti-tank capability, a *Panzerjäger* version was produced (*below*) with an 88 mm. gun. This vehicle proved to be one of the most lethal German weapons of World War II, since it combined the high killing power of the 88 mm. gun with the great mobility of the Panther tank.

terrain is through the application of this linked-vehicle concept. Such a configuration has other advantages; it is easily split down into two or more loads for ease of transportation (particularly by air), and the standardization of a single powered unit means it can be fitted to a whole range of different vehicles. Apart from expense and complication, its main disadvantage lies in its vulnerability.

The steering of a tank is also dependent upon the tracks,

since the tractive effort transferred to the ground is via the tracks. Different tracks have different performances on various terrains, and therefore much research is required in order to select a particular track for general use. At the same time, it must be borne in mind that the tracks must possess

One of the US self-propelled weapons used latterly during World War II was the American tank-destroyer, the M-18 version being illustrated above. In general overall design, this type of vehicle closely resembled a tank, although the subtle difference lay in its inability to carry out the more sophisticated functions of tanks. This vehicle was one of the earliest to utilize torsion-bar suspension.

some level of resistance to projectiles and mines.

One interesting solution to the steering of tracked vehicles was carried out by Dr Merritt in the design of the Tetrarch light tank. Here, instead of varying the speeds of the two tracks, the suspension components were so designed as to adopt the arc of an ellipse at the bottom, and a straight line at the top. When the steering wheel was turned, the top part of the track remained straight, and the bottom half curved in the direction governed by the controls. This system was also used to a minor extent on the Universal carrier and the Second World War German half-tracks. Apart from being very delicate, and therefore vulnerable, the system implied that the driving sprocket and idler wheel should rest on the ground, thereby limiting the step-climbing ability to that of a wheeled vehicle.

One other major consideration in the design of a tracked vehicle is the provision of a smooth ride. This is governed by the suspension system, which is intended to damp-out the

The value of the self-propelled gun in modern-day armies fluctuates greatly. Apart from mobile missile carriers and special anti-aircraft vehicles, the Russians today use only one model of self-propelled artillery. This vehicle is the ASU-85 (*below*) and is a special airborne 85 mm. gun motor carriage employing components of the PT-76 light amphibious tank, although it has no inborn amphibious capability itself.

(*Right*) one of the special artillery versions of the French AMX-13 light tank. This is quite a feat of modern engineering since it mounts a powerful 155 mm. field howitzer on such a light chassis. Because of its light weight, the vehicle can even be air-lifted by certain types of helicopters. The high recoil energy of the gun is absorbed by the special spade trails hydraulically lowered from the rear of the vehicle.

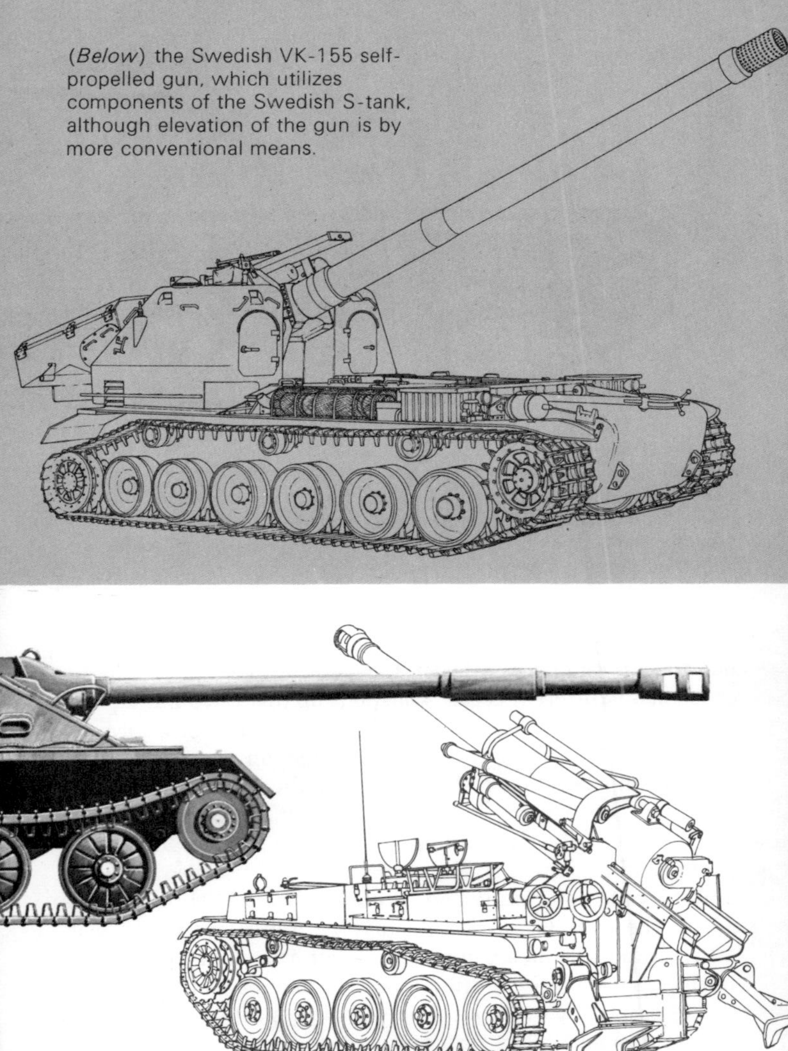

(*Below*) the Swedish VK-155 self-propelled gun, which utilizes components of the Swedish S-tank, although elevation of the gun is by more conventional means.

Many nations produce their light self-propelled guns on the basis of their contemporary armoured personnel carriers. The German *Panzerjäger K* (above) is one such vehicle. It is based on the HS-30 carrier and mounts a 90 mm. gun. Due to the special method of mounting the gun the vehicle is very low.

vibrations of the vehicle caused through rapid changes in terrain configuration. The faster the system is able to damp-out the vibrations, the faster the vehicle may travel. There are so many different types of suspension that it would require a separate book in itself to discuss them all. The best form of suspension is, undoubtedly, the air cushion; no mechanical suspension has yet been able to provide the excellent damping effects of this system. The best mechanical system so far developed is the hydro-pneumatic type, which not only provides the smoothest ride across country, but also allows a tank to vary its attitude and ground clearance. Through this means the overall tank height may be minimized (making it difficult to hit), and a firmer firing platform may be provided. In the same way, the ground clearance may be increased to an extent where the hull may clear a large proportion of expected terrain obstacles. This system is still under development, but at the moment has two major disadvantages. Firstly, it is too vulnerable to attack (by reason of its complication), and secondly it takes up too much room inside the tank.

Prior to the introduction of the hydro-pneumatic type, the

The British also utilize their FV-432 armoured personnel carrier chassis as a basis for a light-weight self-propelled 105 mm. field howitzer. This vehicle (*below*) is called the Abbot and has a special collapsible screen enabling easy flotation across inland waterways. Water propulsion is via the tracks.

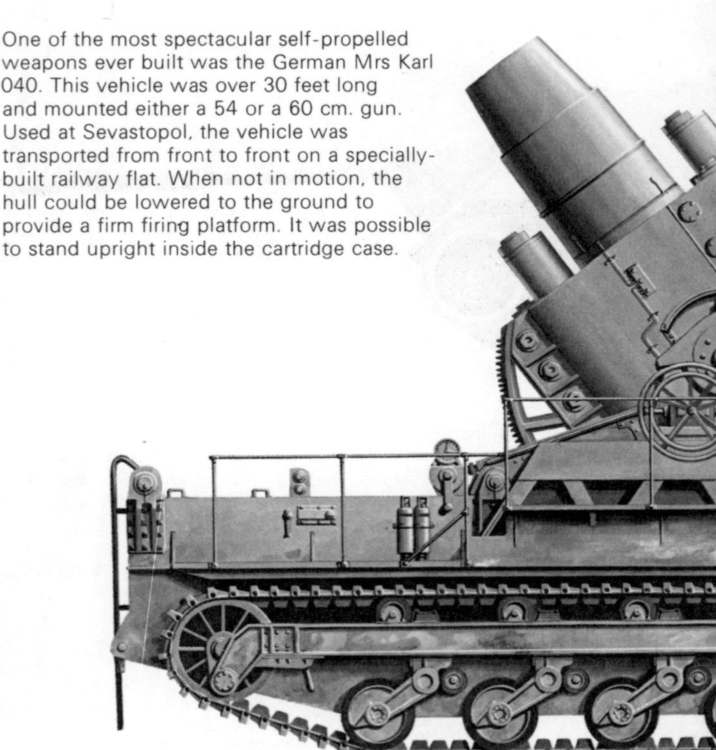

One of the most spectacular self-propelled weapons ever built was the German Mrs Karl 040. This vehicle was over 30 feet long and mounted either a 54 or a 60 cm. gun. Used at Sevastopol, the vehicle was transported from front to front on a specially-built railway flat. When not in motion, the hull could be lowered to the ground to provide a firm firing platform. It was possible to stand upright inside the cartridge case.

best available suspension system was the interleaved design used by the Germans on the Panther tank. This was, however, extremely complicated, not only taking up too much room within the tank, but also demanding a major overhaul every time a torsion-bar broke or a road wheel was shot off. One interesting point concerning this type of suspension is connected with German experience in Russia. The Russians discovered that, during the early hours of the morning, these overlapping bogie wheels were often welded together by ice, thus rendering the vehicles immobile. In typical Russian fashion, this was the time they decided to attack.

The majority of British tanks built so far have used one of

two types of suspension – the Christie or Horstmann types. The Christie suspension is a very famous type designed by the American tank pioneer W. J. Christie during the late 1920s. It was first put into practice by the Russians, who continued to utilize it on all their medium tank models right up to the T–34. The main drawback with the Christie type suspension is that it occupies too much room inside the tank and is too vulnerable to fire. The Horstmann type, on the other hand, is not a particularly good suspension, but it is very robust; each suspension unit is self-contained and bolted directly to the tank hull, and consequently occupies no room within the tank. It also greatly reduces difficulties of maintenance and replacement.

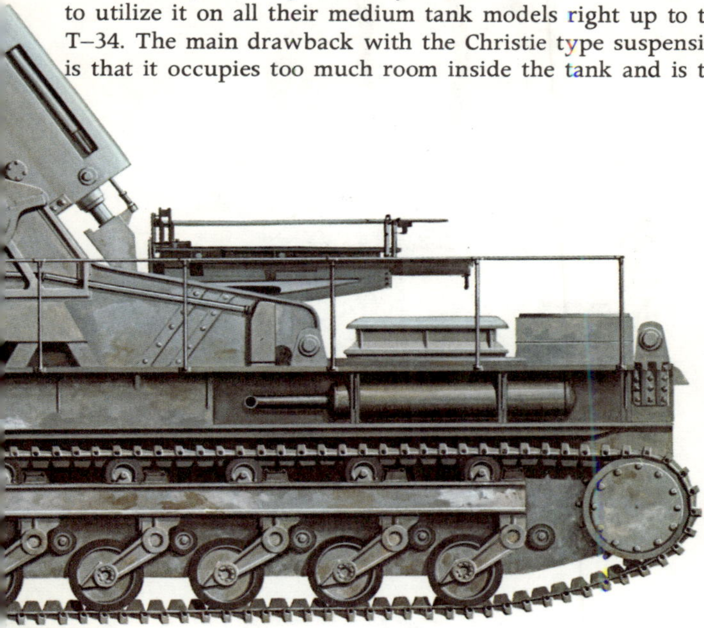

The last major branch of tank technology is that associated with the engine, but since tank engines differ very little from conventional commercial models, there is very little to say. Generally, they should have practically square cylinder head dimensions and lack bulk.

Originally, tanks were powered by internal combustion

One special function of self-propelled artillery was defence against air attack. Because of the air superiority achieved by the Allies towards the end of the war, the Germans were compelled to delegate a proportion of their tank chassis to use for air defence. Above is shown the 'Whirlwind', a special anti-aircraft conversion of the Pz.Kpfw.IV medium tank. (*Right*) one of the most effective Soviet artillery vehicles was the SU-100. A powerful 100 mm. anti-tank gun was mounted in a special casemate on the T-34 medium tank chassis. The revolutionary design in this type of vehicle markedly influenced German SP development.

spark-ignition engines, although several types were made with steam engines. The most significant stage in the development of tank engines was the swing to diesels. The diesel engine possessed two advantages over the petrol type – firstly, diesel fuel does not present such a fire hazard as petrol; and secondly, diesel engines provide a far greater range of operation for one filling of fuel. Although the diesel is still in general use with tanks today, a few countries, including Britain, are pioneering the multi-fuel engine. This engine is essentially a compression-ignition type, but has the ability to run on several types of fuel, thereby reducing logistic problems. With the exception of the Swedish, no army today makes extensive use of the gas-turbine engine, although Britain, France and the USA have constructed prototypes of tanks driven by this type of engine. Even in the Swedish vehicles this forms only the subsidiary power plant, and they use it because of its cold-starting qualities. Due to the reduction in moving parts, the gas-turbine obtains greater energy from fuel and is more reliable.

Tank heraldry:
(*Top left*) Le Régiment Blindé de Fusiliers Marins
(*Top right*) United States 7th Cavalry
(*Centre left*) Great Britain 1st Armoured Division
(*Centre right*) Great Britain 7th Armoured Division
(*Bottom left*) Red Army Guard insignia
(*Bottom right*) Marking to be found on many Japanese tanks

Tank heraldry:
(*Top left*) 12th Panzer Division
(*Top right*) 17th Panzer Division
(*Centre left*) Gross Deutschland Panzer Grenadier Division
(*Centre right*) 24th Panzer Division
(*Bottom left*) Afrika Korps
(*Bottom right*) 21st Panzer Division

(*Above*) the Italian Semovente 75/18, the most common Italian self-propelled gun of the Second World War. It was based on the chassis of the M.13/40 medium, the word 'Semovente' being Italian for 'self-propelled mounting'. Much use was made of this vehicle in the Western Desert. The main armament was a low-velocity 75 mm. gun. Like most other nations, the Italians produced a large number of self-propelled mountings for various types of weapons. (*Below*) the British Churchill Crocodile. This was a special flame-throwing version of the Churchill tank. The flame-projector was mounted in the hull front next to the driver (the position usually adopted by a machine-gun). Fuel and pressure systems were fitted in the special trailer towed behind the vehicle. After flame fuel was expended the tank could release the trailer and use its 75 mm. gun as normal.

FUTURE TRENDS

There are a number of possible fields of research which might well enhance the effectiveness of the tank in future war. The possible developments of firepower are virtually unlimited; research into recoilless weapons is well under way, and the guided missile has under no circumstances reached its final configuration. Although there are present disadvantages in the employment of guided missiles, arising primarily from technical difficulties, it is not difficult to visualize these being overcome. Since the chemical energy warhead has better armour-piercing qualities than the kinetic-energy type, and due to its high-explosive capability, the guided-missile might present a solution to the round-selection problem. As a compromise, the chemical-energy guided weapon would allow the use of automatic loaders, and it should not require much effort to provide a separate-loading guided weapon for ease of stowage and handling. If the speed of the missile can be increased substantially, at the same time retaining the facility to 'home', or be controlled in flight, then it might take the place of the conventional gun mounting.

Armour is a field which proves to be completely unpredictable; there are a number of materials and techniques which may be applied to the armouring of vehicles, but in the meantime steel armour proves to be the most efficient. The existence of kinetic-energy armour-piercing projectiles forces the tank designer to adopt 'weight-consuming' steel armour, since it is only this expedient which will provide any degree of immunity from this form of attack. In the case of chemical-energy attack, there are a number of 'devices' or tricks which can be used to save weight of armour.

It seems that the field in which most efforts are being made

is that of mobility. Reference has already been made to the advances which are being made with regard to tank suspension systems but, at present, the conventional mechanical suspensions remain the most suitable. Mobility of tanks has remained almost stagnant for the past two decades, whereas the other characteristics – firepower and armour protection – have been improved significantly. The Americans are currently experimenting with a vehicle known as the Airoll, which has a good performance in almost any type of environment – including swamps and water. Generally its configuration resembles closely that of a conventional tracked vehicle but, in place of the normal webbed tracks, there are special tracks which have air-filled rollers in place of steel links. In this manner the vehicle runs along a series of pneumatic rollers which provide flotation in soft loam or water. One of the initial problems with this design was the vulnerability of the pneumatic rollers to small-arms fire. However, experiments with special rollers, filled with such materials as plastics and polystyrene, have

(*Left*) an interesting conversion of the French AMX-13 light tank (illustrated on page 62). In order to amplify the anti-tank capability, lethal anti-tank missiles are mounted on the turret front above the gun. Usually, three or four missiles are carried and these may be launched individually. The missiles usually have either a HESH or a shaped-charge warhead and are guided towards the target. Directional control of the missiles is achieved through a fine wire which is reeled out like a fishing-line as the missile progresses. The missile may be steered by rudders or moveable jet nozzles. Some missiles operate by radio-control.

shown that this problem may be overcome. The major problem in this design is, however, bulk. The use of these special rollers makes the vehicle very high. Even if the design proves unsuitable for tank use, it will certainly have great application as an amphibious assault carrier and lends itself admirably to the particular climatic conditions of Vietnam and similar environments.

A field which has not yet been applied directly to armoured fighting vehicles, but may well be in the near future, is that of walking machines. The Americans have developed a series of highly sophisticated walking machines which are controlled by electronic amplification of the operator's muscular power. A four-legged vehicle may be easily controlled by a man using his arms and legs; he 'rides' the vehicle in a similar fashion to a bicycle, only pedalling with his hands as well. The best form of walking vehicle would be one with six or eight legs, for if we scaled up the mobility of a spider the results would prove amazing. A spider can achieve a scale speed of close to

100 mph across a mini-mountain range and, although this would not necessarily prove possible at larger scales, the mobility of a fighting vehicle could be improved substantially. Fortunately, motivation of this line of development stems from its application in another important field – the exploration of extra-terrestial bodies. Since this field, and the National Defence Field, represent a major proportion of the American

Due to the relatively low strategic speed of tanks, and the wear and tear incurred through prolonged motoring, such vehicles are usually transported from front to front by special transporters. The vehicle shown above was a standard model employed by the Allies during the Second World War and was manufactured by the American Diamond T company. Special ramps are attached to the rear of the vehicle to facilitate easy loading, and a winch is provided to haul

research budget, it is highly probable that development of these walking machines will receive a high priority.

It must be appreciated that the above outline of factors influencing tank design is only a rough one. The development of a tank today is a highly complex task and is undertaken by whole teams of engineers and scientists working on various individual aspects.

damaged tanks on to the platform. The most economic method of moving tanks around is by rail but often, as in the Western desert, rail systems are non-existent and sometimes congestion can occur. Then again, rail networks are predictable routes and may often be vulnerable from the air. For amphibious operations, tanks are carried in special tank landing ships, called LSTs (Landing ships, Tank). The tank being transported above is an American Sherman with a 75 mm. gun.

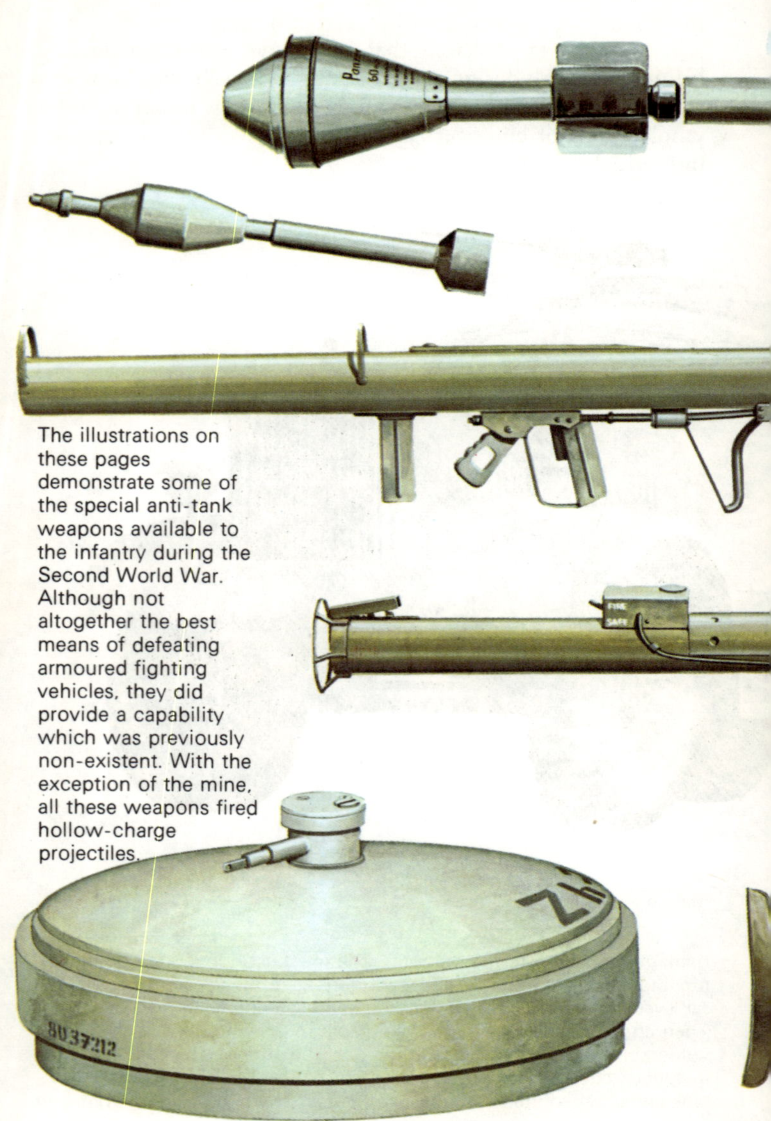

The illustrations on these pages demonstrate some of the special anti-tank weapons available to the infantry during the Second World War. Although not altogether the best means of defeating armoured fighting vehicles, they did provide a capability which was previously non-existent. With the exception of the mine, all these weapons fired hollow-charge projectiles.

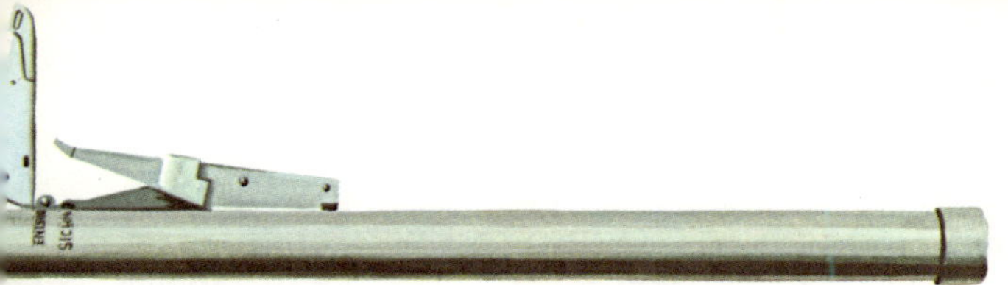

The three upper illustrations show rocket-propelled weapons launched from hand-held tubes. These were developed by the Germans, Americans and the Russians. The types illustrated in the centre are often referred to as 'Bazookas'.

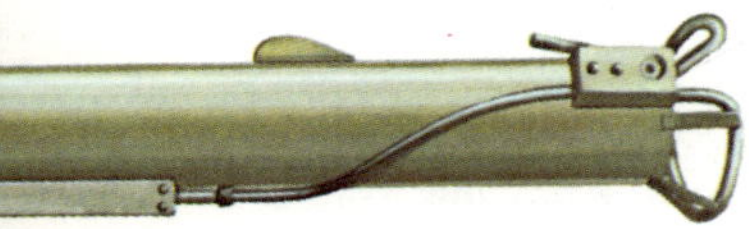

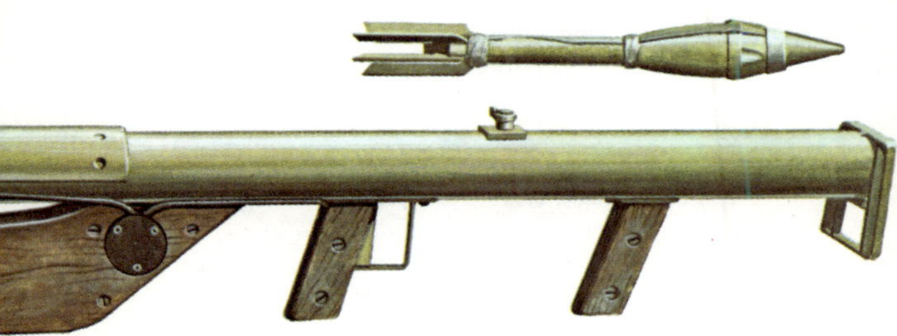

The anti-tank mine (*left*) is self-explanatory, but the PIAT projector (*below*) is quite novel. The shaped-charge missile is launched by means of a powerful spring, which is cocked in a similar manner to that of an air-gun.

BOOKS TO READ

British and American Tanks of World War II by P. Chamberlain and C. Ellis; Arms and Armour Press, London, 1969.

Armoured Fighting Vehicles of the World by C. Foss; Ian Allan, London, 1971.

Tanks in the Great War by Major General J. F. C. Fuller; John Murray, London, 1920.

Panzer Leader by General Heinz Guderian; Michael Joseph, London, 1952.

Tank Warfare by K. Macksey; Rupert Hart-Davis, London, 1971.

Tank by K. Macksey and J. H. Batchelor; Macdonald Unit 75, London, 1970.

Wozy Bojowe (Combat Vehicles) by J. Magnuski; Wydawnictwo Ministerstwa Obrony Narodwej, Warsaw, 1960 and 1964.

Panzer Battles by Major General F. W. von Mellenthin; Cassell and Co., London, 1955.

Russian Tanks 1900–1970 by J. F. Milsom; Arms and Armour Press, London, 1970.

Armoured Forces by R. M. Ogorkiewicz; Arms and Armour Press, London, 1970.

Design and Development of Fighting Vehicles by R. M. Ogorkiewicz; Macdonald, London, 1968.

The Tank by D. Orgill; Heinemann, London, 1970.

Tanks in Battle by Colonel H. C. B. Rogers OBE; Seeley Service Co., London, 1965.

Die Deutschen Panzer (The German Tank) by Dr. F. M. Senger von Etterlin; J. F. Lehmanns Verlag, München, 1965. (English edition by Arms and Armour Press, London, 1969.)

Taschenbuch der Panzer by Dr F. M. Senger von Etterlin; (various editions), J. F. Lehmanns Verlag, München.

Machine Age Armies by J. Wheldon; Abelard Schuman, London, 1968.

ARMOUR IN PROFILE Series – individual pamphlets on armoured fighting vehicles; Profile Publications Limited, Windsor.

ARMOR SERIES – booklets covering World War II armoured fighting vehicles; Aero Publishers Inc., Fallbrook, California, USA.

BELLONA MILITARY VEHICLE PRINTS AND HANDBOOKS – collections of photographs, data and drawings of military vehicles; Model and Allied Publications Limited, London.

INDEX

SOME OTHER TITLES IN THIS SERIES

- Arts
- Domestic Animals and Pets
- Domestic Science
- Gardening
- General Information
- History and Mythology
- Natural History
- Popular Science

Arts
Antique Furniture/Architecture/Clocks and Watches/Glass for Collectors/Jewellery/Musical Instruments/Porcelain/Victoriana

Domestic Animals and Pets
Budgerigars/Cats/Dog Care/Dogs/Horses and Ponies/Pet Birds/Pets for Children/Tropical Freshwater Aquaria/Tropical Marine Aquaria

Domestic Science
Flower Arranging

Gardening
Chrysanthemums/Garden Flowers/Garden Shrubs/House Plants/Plants for Small Gardens/Roses

General Information
Aircraft/Arms and Armour/Coins and Medals/Flags/Guns/Military Uniforms/National Costumes of the world/Rockets and Missiles/Sailing/Sailing Ships and Sailing Craft/Sea Fishing/Trains/Veteran and Vintage Cars/Warships

History and Mythology
Age of Shakespeare/Archaeology/Discovery of: Africa/The American West/Australia/Japan/North America/South America/Myths and Legends of: Africa/Ancient Egypt/Ancient Greece/Ancient Rome/India/The South Seas/Witchcraft and Black Magic

Natural History
The Animal Kingdom/Animals of Australia and New Zealand/Animals of Southern Asia/Bird Behaviour/Birds of Prey/Butterflies/Evolution of Life/Fishes of the world/Fossil Man/A Guide to the Seashore/ Life in the Sea/Mammals of the world/Monkeys and Apes/Natural History Collecting/The Plant Kingdom/Prehistoric Animals/Seabirds/Seashells/Snakes of the world/Trees of the World/Tropical Birds/Wild Cats

Popular Science
Astronomy/Atomic Energy/Chemistry/Computers at Work/The Earth/Electricity/Electronics/Exploring the Planets/The Human Body/Mathematics/Microscopes and Microscopic Life/Undersea Exploration/The Weather Guide